TURBO C++

Other Titles of Interest

TURBO C++

IRA POHL

University of California

Santa Cruz

The Benjamin/Cummings Publishing Company, Inc.

Redwood City, California ■ Fort Collins, Colorado
Menlo Park, California ■ Reading, Massachusetts ■ New York
Don Mills, Ontario ■ Wokingham, U.K. ■ Amsterdam ■ Bonn
Sydney ■ Singapore ■ Tokyo ■ Madrid ■ San Juan

Sponsoring Editor: John Thompson
Editing, Design, and Production: Larry Olsen
Cover Design: Juan Vargas
Composition: Ocean View Technical Publications

Turbo C ++ is a trademark of Borland International, Inc.
UNIX is a trademark of AT&T Bell Laboratories.
MS-DOS is a trademark of Microsoft, Inc.

Library of Congress Cataloging-in-Publication Data
Pohl, Ira
    Turbo C++ / Ira Pohl.
        p.   cm.
    Includes bibliographical references and index.
    ISBN 0-8053-6017-4
    1. C++ (Computer Program language)   2. Turbo C++ (Computer
program)   I. Title.
    QA76.73.C153P66   1991
    005.26'2--dc20   90-47003
                                                      CIP

ISBN 0-8053-6017-4

ABCDEFGHIJ-MA-9543210

The Benjamin/Cummings Publishing Company, Inc.
390 Bridge Parkway
Redwood City, California 94065

FOREWORD

Object-Oriented Programming (OOP) is the programming technology for the 1990s. C++ is increasingly the OOP language of choice for educators and programming professionals. Turbo C++ continues Borland's tradition of providing affordable quality compilers to the educational community. Borland's Turbo C++ provides support within an integrated development environment for learning and using this technology.

There is an urgent need for a textbook that presents C++ to students and professionals and introduces them to the elegant technology of the Turbo environment. Ira Pohl has met this need in superior style with *TURBO C++*.

The book is an outstanding introduction to programming in Turbo C++ for the programmer or student already familiar with C. The approach is an evolutionary teaching process with C as a starting point and allows the reader to immediately use Turbo C++ to advantage.

Turbo C++ combines a powerful development environment with the C++ language and library. By carefully developing working Turbo C++ programs, using the method of *dissection*, this book presents a simple and thorough introduction to the programming process in Turbo C++. All the major pieces of code were tested using Borland's Turbo C++.

For the beginner a simple introduction to the Turbo C language is *Turbo C: The Essentials of C Programming* by Al Kelley and Ira Pohl (Benjamin/Cummings, 1988). As a package, the two books offer an integrated treatment of the C and C++ programming languages and their use.

Turbo C++ is a total environment for developing C and C++ software. It provides the user with an unparalleled *Integrated Development Environment (IDE)*. Students will find that *TURBO C++* by Ira Pohl is the gateway to the successful mastery of programming in Borland's Turbo C++.

Philippe Kahn
Chairman, President, and CEO
Borland International, Inc.

PREFACE

This book is intended as an introduction to programming in Turbo C++ for the programmer or student already familiar with C. Its approach is to use an evolutionary teaching process with C as a starting point. The programmer can stop and use the language facilities up to that point in the text. We start with C and end with C++. The book is a tutorial on Turbo C++ programming.

C++ is a powerful modern successor language to C. Turbo C++ combines a powerful development environment with the AT&T Release 2.0 version of C++. C++ was invented at Bell Labs by Bjarne Stroustrup in the mid-1980s. C++ adds to C the concept of *class*, a mechanism for providing user-defined types also called *abstract data types*. It supports *object-oriented programming* (OOP) by these means and by providing inheritance and run-time type binding. C is the present; C++ is the future.

By carefully developing example C++ programs, using the method of *dissection*, this book presents a simple and thorough introduction to the programming process in C++. Dissection is a technique for explaining new elements in a program that the student is seeing for the first time. It highlights key points in the many examples of working code that are used to teach by example.

This book is intended for use in a first course in programming in C++. It can be used as a supplementary text in an advanced programming course, data structures course, software methodology course, comparative language course, or other courses where the instructor wants C++ to be the language of choice. Each chapter presents a number of carefully explained programs. Many programs and functions are dissected.

All the major pieces of code were tested. A consistent and proper coding style is adopted from the beginning. The style standard used is one chosen by professionals in the C++ community.

For the programmer who has no C experience, this book should be used in conjunction with *A Book on C,* Second Edition, by Al Kelley and Ira Pohl (Benjamin/Cummings, 1990). As a package, the two books offer an integrated treatment of the C and C++ programming languages and their use that is unavailable elsewhere. For the beginner a simple introduction to the Turbo C language is *Turbo C: The Essentials of C Programming* by Al Kelley and Ira Pohl (Benjamin/Cummings, 1988).

Each chapter has:

Turbo C++ Considerations. Turbo C++ is a total environment for developing C and C++ software. It provides the user with an unparalleled *Integrated Development Environment (IDE)*. Turbo C++ is based on Release 2.0 of the C++ language. This section emphasizes features that are novel and distinct for Turbo C++. It also tries to be helpful in explaining language issues that are system-dependent or very recently changed from older C++ language implementations.

Dissections. Programs that are particularly illustrative of the themes of a chapter are analyzed in special dissection sections. Dissection is similar to a structured walk-through of the code. Its intention is to explain to the reader newly encountered programming elements and idioms.

Summary. A succinct list of points covered in each chapter is presented at the end of the chapter as a helpful review.

Exercises. The exercises test the student's knowledge of the language. Many exercises are intended to be done interactively while reading the text. This encourages self-paced instruction by the reader. The exercises also frequently extend the reader's knowledge to an advanced area of use.

The book incorporates:

An Evolutionary Approach. The C programmer can immediately benefit from programming in Turbo C++. The early chapters show how the language is improved by stronger typing, a new comment style, call-by-reference, and other useful minor additions. The middle chapters show how classes work. Classes are the basis for abstract data types and object-oriented programming. Again the student starts from C and moves to C++. The later chapters give advanced details of the use of inheritance and stream I/O. At any point in the text, the programmer can stop and apply the new material.

Teaching by Example.   The book is a tutorial that stresses examples of working code. Right from the start, the student is introduced to full working programs. An interactive environment is assumed. Exercises are integrated with the examples to encourage experimentation. Excessive detail is avoided in explaining the larger elements of writing working code. Each chapter has several important example programs. Major elements of these programs are explained by the method of dissection.

Data Structures in C++.   The text emphasizes many of the standard data structures from computer science. Stacks, safe arrays, dynamically allocated multidimensional arrays, lists, trees, and strings are all implemented. Exercises extend the student's understanding of how to implement and use these structures. Implementation is consistent with an abstract-data-type approach to software.

Object-Oriented Programming.   The reader is led gradually to the object-oriented style. Chapter 0 and Chapter 1 discuss how the C programmer can benefit in important ways from a switch to C++ and object-oriented programming. The terminology of object-oriented concepts is defined, and the ways these concepts are supported by C++ are introduced. Chapter 3 introduces classes, which are the basic mechanism for producing modular programs and implementing abstract data types. Class variables are the *objects* being manipulated. Chapter 6 develops inheritance and virtual functions, two key elements in this paradigm. Chapter 8 integrates all the previous techniques and shows how to properly write multicomponent programs in an object-oriented style. The subtleties of OOP are a consequence of a *Platonic* programming philosophy. This book develops and transforms the programmer to appreciate this point of view.

C++ Release 2.0 and *iostream.h*.   C++ continues to change at a rapid pace for such a widely used language. This book is based on the most recent standard: AT&T Release 2.0 and its associated libraries. The examples use the *iostream.h* I/O library, which has begun to replace the older *stream.h* and *stdio.h* libraries. The book attempts to stay with mainstream aspects of the language that are most likely to remain standard in future releases. It avoids arcane features of the language that are error prone or confusing.

Acknowledgments

My special thanks go to my wife, Debra Dolsberry, who encouraged me throughout this project. She acted as technical editor and implemented and tested all major pieces of code. Her careful implementations of the code and Exercises often led to important improvements. Others who provided helpful suggestions and encouragement include: Nan Borreson, Borland International; Skona Brittain; Al Conrad; Steve Demurjian; Samuel Druker, Zortech Limited; Robert Durling; Bruce Eckel; Daniel Edelson; Gene Fisher; Robert Hansen, Lattice, Incorporated; John Hardin, Hewlett-Packard, Incorporated; Al Kelley; Jim Kempf, Sun Microsystems, Incorporated; Ellen Mickanin; Laura Pohl, Cottage Consultants; and Linda Werner. In addition, my editors Alan Apt and Jean Foltz were very supportive. Finally, I thank Bjarne Stroustrup for inventing such an elegant language and encouraging others to help develop and teach it.

Ira Pohl
University of California
Santa Cruz

CONTENTS

3

CLASSES   63

4 CONSTRUCTORS AND DESTRUCTORS   91

5 OPERATOR OVERLOADING AND CONVERSIONS   119

6 INHERITANCE   149

7 INPUT/OUTPUT   179

8 ADVANCED FEATURES   201

To My Students

Chapter 0

Object-Oriented Programming in Turbo C++

C++ was created by Bjarne Stroustrup in the early 1980s. Stroustrup had two main goals: (1) C++ was to be compatible with ordinary C, and (2) it was to extend C using the class construct of Simula 67. The class construct is an extension of the C `struct`. The language, in an early form, is described in B. Stroustrup, *The C++ Programming Language* [1]. Important additions to the current language are described in B. Stroustrup, *The Evolution of C++: 1985 to 1987* [2].

This book teaches C++ to programmers already familiar with C [3]. It does this by building from C to C++. Two aspects of C++ as a successor language to C are stressed. The first is C++'s superiority to C as a general-purpose programming language because of its new features. The second is the success of C++ as an *object-oriented* programming language. In the next section we define what this new concept means.

A major premise of our approach is that C++ is a superior C, even not taking into consideration the extensions to classes. We expect that C++ will replace C as a general-purpose programming language. With C++ the C programmer can improve on ordinary C code in a number of ways that will be illustrated in Chapters 1 and 2.

0.1 Object-Oriented Programming

We will be using the terms *abstract data type (ADT)* and *object-oriented programming (OOP)* to refer to a powerful new programming approach. An ADT is a user-defined extension to the existing types available in the language. It consists of a set of values and a collection of operations that can act on those values. For example, C does not have a complex number type, but C++ provides the class construct to add such a type and integrate it with existing types. *Objects* are class variables. Object-oriented programming allows ADTs to be easily created and used. OOP uses the mechanism of *inheritance* to conveniently derive a new type from an existing user-defined type. It allows the programmer to model the objects found in the problem domain by programming their content and behavior with a class.

The new class construct in C++ provides the *encapsulation* mechanism to implement ADTs. Encapsulation packages both the internal implementation details of the type and the externally available operations and functions that can act on objects of that type. The implementation details can be made inaccessible to client code that uses the type. For example, stack might be implemented as a fixed-length array, while the publicly available operations would include push and pop. Changing the internal implementation to a linked list should not affect how push and pop are used externally. The implementation of stack is hidden from its clients. The details of how to provide data hiding in classes are introduced in Chapter 1 and developed thoroughly in Chapters 3 and 6.

0.2 Why C++ Is a Better C

Since C++ is based on C, it retains much of that language, including a rich operator set, nearly orthogonal design, terseness, and extensibility. C++ is a highly portable language, and translators for it exist on many different machines and systems. C++ compilers are highly compatible with existing C programs because maintaining such compatibility was a design objective. Unlike other object-oriented languages, such as Smalltalk, C++ is an extension of an existing language in wide use on many machines.

If C++ is viewed as an object-oriented language alternative to Smalltalk, it is a relatively inexpensive alternative. Programming in C++ does not require a graphics environment, and C++ programs do not incur run-time expense from type checking or garbage collection.

C++ improves on C in significant ways, especially in supporting strong typing. The function prototype syntax, as now required by ANSI C [4,5], is a C++ innovation. In general, C++ has stronger type rules than C, which makes it a safer language.

C++ is a marriage of the low level with the high level. As Stroustrup states [1], "C is at the machine level, while C++ is at the problem domain level." The user can write code at the level appropriate to the problem while still maintaining contact with the machine-level implementation details.

Operators can be given new definitions based on the types of their arguments. This operator overloading supports the implementation of new types that may be operated upon transparently. Normal functions, like operators, may be overloaded.

There is less reliance on the preprocessor. C programs often use the preprocessor to implement constants and useful macros. However, parameterized `#define` macros introduce insecurities. In C++, the `inline` keyword requests the compiler to compile a function as a macro. This preserves type checking while increasing run-time performance as compared with normal functions. Reliance on the preprocessor is further diminished by the `const` type modifier, which specifies that an object is read-only.

There are a large number of other improvements. A favorite of programmers is the addition of the `//` symbol for one-line comments. There is also a convenient new I/O library. The *iostream.h* library provides a very useful alternative to *stdio.h*. The `new` and `delete` operators provide convenient access to free store.

Abstract data types are implemented in C++ through the `class` mechanism. Classes allow a programmer to control the visibility of the underlying implementation. What is public is accessible and what is private is hidden. Data hiding is one component of object-oriented programming. Classes have member functions, including those that overload operators. Member functions allow the programmer to code the appropriate functionality for the ADT. Classes can be defined through an inheritance mechanism that allows for improved code sharing and library development. Inheritance is another hallmark of object-oriented programming.

C is often criticized as a weakly typed unsafe language [6]. However, C++ is strongly typed. Conversions between types are allowed, provided they are well defined. In fact, the language allows the programmer to create conversion functions between arbitrary types.

Parameter passing in C is unchecked with regard to type or number of actual parameters. This leads to bugs that the compiler cannot catch. In C++, function prototypes allow functions to be fully checked as to count and type. Functions taking variable types or numbers of arguments are also supported. The addition of function prototypes is an aid to the programmer, bringing into the compiler checking that was previously obtainable only through *lint*.

The C array model is pointer-based and one-dimensional without bounds checking. This lack of multidimensional arrays means the programmer must spend more time and effort implementing them using the one-dimensional storage mapping function that is C's paradigm. Development and use of dynamic arrays also require significant work and are not supported in the language. C++ retains the array handling of C; however, classes provide a satisfactory means of transparently implementing general arrays. Multidimensional, dynamic, and bounds-checked arrays can be implemented in libraries.

By and large, the semantics of C++ are much more stringently defined than those of C. For example, type conversion and typing are more carefully implemented. The C need for preprocessor extensibility is curtailed: Function overloading and `inline` can be used to replace macros with arguments, and the `const` type modifier is sufficient for most named constants. The preprocessor's primary remaining uses are file inclusion and conditional compilation.

0.3 Why Switch to Turbo C++?

Turbo C++ supports an advanced integrated programming environment on most DOS and OS/2 machines. This environment is the best single reason to use Borland's Turbo C++. It increases programming productivity over traditional batch and workstation environments that are not integrated. The Borland Turbo C++ system provides a modern debugger, window manager, and project manager. It also supports ANSI C [3, 4].

C++ supports the object-oriented programming style. A chief cost is the increased complexity of the language. (Given C++'s objectives, this is hardly surprising.) Although the benefits gained by living within the C family and adding improved interface schemes outweigh this cost, the complexity that C++ adds to the C language is one of its biggest drawbacks. This complexity reflects the large number of needed new ideas but makes mastery more difficult. To overcome this problem, this book approaches the learning process by gradually transforming the C programmer into a practiced C++ programmer. Each chapter extends from the previous chapter the range of ideas the programmer may use. Each chapter provides additional advice on how to take advantage of the Turbo C++ environment. At any point, the reader can stop and still be partly proficient in C++. In effect, the reader evolves from a standard C programmer to an object-oriented C++ programmer.

C++ is a better C. Turbo C++ is a better programming environment. Turbo C++ is the best widely available, efficient, economical, and comprehensive programming environment. The use of C++ leads to increased convenience in writing code and increased security in the code. Features such as `//` for single line comments, `const` and `inline`, `new` and `delete` for storage management, and call-by-reference parameters simplify the coding process over C. Stronger typing in general, and function prototypes in particular, enhance security and facilitate software methodology.

0.4 References

1. B. Stroustrup, *The C++ Programming Language*, Addison-Wesley, Reading, Mass., 1986. The de facto language reference manual. This book is very difficult reading.

2. B. Stroustrup, The Evolution of C++: 1985 to 1987, in *1987 USENIX C++ Papers*, Sante Fe, N.M., 1987, pp. 1–21. Brings his book up-to-date with version 2 language changes.

3. A. Kelley and I. Pohl, *A Book on C*, Second Edition, Benjamin/Cummings, Menlo Park, Calif., 1990. A comprehensive text on the C programming language. It is written in the style of this book.

4. A. Kelley and I. Pohl, *Turbo C*, Benjamin/Cummings, Menlo Park, Calif., 1988. A tutorial introduction to a popular ANSI C compiler.

5. S. P. Harbison and G. L. Steele, *C: A Reference Manual*, Second Edition, Prentice-Hall, Englewood Cliffs, N.J., 1987. The authoritative reference book on the syntax and semantics of the C programming language.

6. I. Pohl and D. Edelson, A-Z: C Language Shortcomings, *Computer Languages*, vol. 13, no. 2, 1988, pp. 51–64. A brief paper criticizing 26 defects in the original C language.

Chapter 1

An Overview of C++ and Object-Oriented Programming

This chapter gives an overview of the Turbo C++ programming language. It also provides an introduction the use of C++ as an object-oriented programming language. Like the rest of the book, it assumes a knowledge of the C programming language. In the chapter a series of programs is presented, and the elements of each program are carefully explained. The programs increase in complexity, and the examples in the later sections illustrate some of the concepts of object-oriented programming. This approach should give the student a sense of how the language works.

Each feature of C++ is explained briefly. Later chapters will explain each new concept in detail. The examples in this chapter give simple, immediate, hands-on experience with key features of the C++ language. The chapter introduces the reader to stream I/O, operator and function overloading, reference parameters, classes, constructors, destructors, and inheritance. The system used is Borland Turbo C++. This is compatible with AT&T C++ Release 2.0.

Object-oriented programming is implemented in the class construct. The `class` construct in C++ is an extension of `struct` in C. The later examples in this chapter illustrate how C++ implements OOP (object-oriented programming) concepts, such as data hiding, ADTs, inheritance, and type hierarchies.

1.1 Output

Programs must communicate to be useful. Our first example is a program that prints on the screen the phrase "C++ is an improved C." The complete program is

```
//A first C++ program illustrating output.

#include <iostream.h>

main()
{
    cout << "C++ is an improved C.\n";
}
```

The program prints on the screen

```
C++ is an improved C.
```

DISSECTION OF THE *advert* PROGRAM

```
//A first C++ program illustrating output.
```

- The double slash `//` is a new comment symbol. The comment runs to the end of the line. The old C bracketing comment symbols `/* */` are still available for multiline comments.

```
#include <iostream.h>
```

- The *iostream.h* header introduces I/O facilities for C++.

```
cout << "C++ is an improved C.\n";
```

- This statement prints to the screen. The identifier `cout` is the name of the standard output stream. The operator `<<` passes the string "C++ is an improved C.\n" to standard out. Used in this way the *output operator* `<<` is referred to as the *put to* or *insertion* operator.

We can rewrite our first program as follows.

```
//A first C++ program illustrating output.

#include <iostream.h>

main()
{
    cout << "C++ is an improved C." << "\n";
}
```

Although it is different from the first version, it produces the same output. Each time the `<<` is used with `cout`, printing continues from the position where it previously left off. In this case the newline character is output after a second use of the put to operator.

1.2 Input

We will write a program to convert to kilometers the distance in miles from the Earth to the moon. In miles this distance is, on average, 238,857 miles. This number is an integer. To convert miles to kilometers, we multiply by the conversion factor 1.609, a real number.

Our conversion program will use variables capable of storing integer values and real values. In C++ all variables must be declared before their use, but unlike in C, they need not be at the head of a block. Declarations may be mixed in with executable statements. Their scope, however, is still the block within which they are declared. Identifiers should be chosen to reflect their use in the program. In this way, they serve as documentation, making the program more readable.

```
//The distance to the moon converted to kilometers.

#include <iostream.h>

main()
{
    const long int moon = 238857;
    cout << "The moon's distance from Earth is " << moon;
    cout << " miles.\n";

    long int moon_kilo;
    moon_kilo = moon * 1.609;
    cout << "In kilometers this is " << moon_kilo;
    cout << " km.\n";
}
```

The output of the program is

```
The moon's distance from Earth is 238857 miles.
In kilometers this is 384320 km.
```

These programs assume a four byte `int`, but on some machines these integer types should be declared `long`.

DISSECTION OF THE *moon* PROGRAM

```
const long int moon = 238857;
```

- The keyword `const` is new in C++. It replaces some uses of the preprocessor command `define` to create named literals. Using this type modifier informs the compiler that the initialized value of `moon` cannot be changed.

```
cout << "The moon's distance from Earth is " << moon;
```

- The stream I/O in C++ can discriminate among a variety of simple values without needing additional formatting information. Here the value of `moon` will be printed as an integer.

```
long int moon_kilo;
moon_kilo = moon * 1.609;
```

- Declarations can occur after executable statements. This allows declarations of variables to be nearer to their use.

Let us write a program that will convert a series of values from miles to kilometers. The program will be interactive. The user will type in a value in miles, and the program will convert this value to kilometers and print it out.

```
//Miles are converted to kilometers.

#include <iostream.h>
const float m_to_k = 1.609;
inline int convert(int mi) { return (mi * m_to_k); }

main()
{
   int miles;

   do {
      cout << "Input distance in miles: ";
      cin >> miles;
      cout << "\nDistance is " << convert(miles) << " km.\n";
   } while (miles > 0);
}
```

This program uses the input stream variable cin, which is normally standard input. The *input operator* >> is called the *get from* or *extraction* operator, which assigns values from the input stream to a variable. This program illustrates both input and output.

DISSECTION OF THE *mi_km* PROGRAM

```
const float m_to_k = 1.609;
inline int convert(int mi) { return (mi * m_to_k); }
```

■ C++ reduces C's traditional reliance on the preprocessor. For example, instead of having to use define, special constants, such as the conversion factor 1.609, are simply assigned to variables specified as constants. The new keyword inline specifies that a function is to be compiled, if possible as a macro. As a rule, inline should be done sparingly and only on short functions. Also note how the parameter mi is declared within the function parentheses. C++ uses *function prototypes* to define and declare functions. This will be explained in the next section.

```
do {
    cout << "Input distance in miles: ";
    cin >> miles;
    cout << "\nDistance is " << convert(miles) << " km.\n";
} while (miles > 0);
```

■ The program repeatedly prompts the user for a distance in miles. The program is terminated by a zero or negative value. The value placed in the standard input stream is automatically converted to an integer value assigned to miles.

1.3 Function Prototypes

The syntax of functions in C++ inspired the new function prototype syntax found in ANSI C compilers. Basically, the types of parameters are listed inside the header parentheses. By explicitly listing the type and number of arguments, strong type checking and assignment-compatible conversions are possible in C++. The following example illustrates these points:

```
//A program illustrating function prototypes.

#include <iostream.h>

main()
{
    int    add3(int, int, int);
    float average(int);
    int    score_1, score_2, score_3, sum;

    cout << "\nEnter 3 scores: ";
    cin >> score_1 >> score_2 >> score_3;
    sum = add3(score_1, score_2, score_3);
    cout << "\nTheir sum is " << sum << ".\n";
    cout << "\nTheir average is " << average(sum) << ".\n";
    sum = add3(1.5 * score_1, score_2, score_3);
    cout << "\nThe weighted sum is " << sum << ".\n";
    cout << "\nTheir average is " << average(sum) << ".\n";
}

int add3(int a, int b, int c)
{
    return (a + b + c);
}

float average(int s)
{
    return (s / 3.0);
}
```

DISSECTION OF THE *add3* PROGRAM

```
int    add3(int, int, int);
float average(int);
```

- ■ These declarations at the head of `main` are function prototypes. They inform the compiler of the type and number of arguments to expect for each externally specified function. The list of arguments can optionally include variable names. So,

  ```
  int add3(int a, int b, int c);
  ```

  is also possible.

```
sum = add3(1.5 * score_1, score_2, score_3);
```

- ■ This would not be correct in traditional C. In traditional C, the first argument `1.5 * score_1` is promoted to `double` and passed unconverted to a local place holder expecting an integer. In C++ this expression is converted to an integer value as per the function prototype specification. This single change markedly improves C++ program reliability over traditional C.

```
int add3(int a, int b, int c)
{
    return (a + b + c);
}
```

- ■ Here is the actual function definition. It could just as well have been imported from another file. It is compatible with the function prototype declaration in `main`.

1.4 Classes and Abstract Data Types

What is truly novel about C++ is its aggregate type `class`, which the language introduces. A `class` is an extension of the idea of `struct` in traditional C. A `class` provides the means for implementing a user-defined data type and associated functions and operators. Therefore a `class` is an implementation of an abstract data type. Let us write a `class` called `string` that will implement a restricted form of string.

```
//An elementary implementation of type string.

#include <string.h>
#include <iostream.h>

const int max_len = 255;

class string {
   char s[max_len];
   int  len;
public:
   void assign(const char* st) { strcpy(s, st); len = strlen(st); }
   int  length() { return (len); }
   void print() { cout << s << "\nLength: " << len << "\n"; }
};
```

Two important additions to the structure concept of traditional C are found in this example: (1) it has members that are functions, such as `assign`, and (2) it has both public and private members. The keyword `public` indicates the visibility of the members that follow it. Without this keyword the members are private to the class. Private members are available for use only by other member functions of the class. Public members are available to any function within the scope of the class declaration. Privacy allows part of the implementation of a class type to be "hidden." This restriction prevents unanticipated modifications to the data structure. Restricted access or *data hiding* is a feature of object-oriented programming.

The declaration of member functions allows the ADT to have particular functions act on its private representation. For example, the member function `length` returns the length of the string defined to be the number of characters up to but excluding the first zero value character. The member function `print` outputs both the string and its length. The member function `assign` stores a character string into the hidden variable `s` and computes and stores its length in the hidden variable `len`.

We can now use this data type `string` as if it were a basic type of the language. It obeys the standard block structure scope rules of C. Other code that uses this type is a *client*. The client can use the public members only to act on objects of type `string`.

```
//Test of the class string.
main()
{
   string  one, two;
   char    three[40] = {"My name is Charles Babbage."};

   one.assign("My name is Alan Turing.");
   two.assign(three);
   cout << three;
   cout << "\nLength: " << strlen(three) << "\n";
   //Print shorter of one and two.
   if (one.length() <= two.length())
      one.print();
   else
      two.print();
}
```

The variables `one` and `two` are of type `string`. The variable `three` is of type pointer to `char` and is not compatible with `string`. The member functions are called using the dot operator or "structure member operator." As is seen from their definitions, these member functions act on the hidden private member fields of the named variables. One cannot write inside `main` the expression `one.len` expecting to access this member. The output of this example program is

```
My name is Charles Babbage.
Length: 27
My name is Alan Turing.
Length: 23
```

1.5 Overloading

The term *overloading* refers to the practice of giving several meanings to an operator or a function. The meaning selected depends on the types of the arguments used by the operator or function. Let us overload the function `print` in the previous example. This will be a second definition of the `print` function.

```
void print(const char* c)
{
   cout << c << "\nLength is " << strlen(c) << "\n";
}
```

This version of `print` takes a single argument of type pointer to `char`. The argument `c` is declared `const`, meaning that the character values pointed to by `c` are not changed by `print()`. Unlike the original version, it is not a member function. We can modify `main` by deleting the two lines

```
cout << three;
cout << "\nLength: " << strlen(three) << "\n";
```

from the previous example and replacing them with a call to `print`:

```
print(three);
```

It is also possible to overload most of the standard C operators. For example, let us overload + to mean concatenate two strings. To do this we need to introduce two new keywords: `friend` and `operator`. The keyword `operator` introduces the operator token and replaces what would otherwise be a function name in a function declaration. The keyword `friend` gives a function access to the private members of a class variable. A `friend` function is not a member of the class but has the privileges of a member function in the class in which it is declared.

```
//Overloading the function print and the operator + .

#include <string.h>
#include <iostream.h>

const int max_len = 255;

class string {
   char s[max_len];
   int  len;
public:
   void assign(const char* st) { strcpy(s, st); len = strlen(st); }
   int  length() { return (len); }
   void print() { cout << s << "\nLength: " << len << "\n"; }
   friend string operator +(const string& a, const string& b);
};
```

```
string operator +(const string& a, const string& b)    //overload +
{
   string temp;

   temp.assign(a.s);
   temp.len = a.len + b.len;
   if (temp.len < max_len)
      strcat(temp.s, b.s);
   else
      cerr << "Max length exceeded in concatenation.\n";
   return (temp);
}

void print(const char* c)
{
   cout << c << "\nLength: " << strlen(c) << "\n";
}


main()
{
   string    one, two, both;
   char      three[40] = {"My name is Charles Babbage."};

   one.assign("My name is Alan Turing.");
   two.assign(three);
   print(three);           //one form of print
   //Print shorter of one and two.
   if (one.length() <= two.length())
      one.print();         //member function form of print
   else
      two.print();
   both = one + two;       //plus overloaded to be concatenate
   both.print();
}
```

DISSECTION OF THE *operator +* FUNCTION

```
string operator +(const string& a, const string& b)
```

■ Plus is overloaded. The two arguments it will take are both
strings. The arguments are "called by reference." The declaration
type& identifier declares the identifier to be a reference variable.
Use of const indicates that the arguments cannot be modified.

This extension to traditional C allows call-by-reference as found in languages such as Pascal.

```
string temp;
```

■ The function needs to return a value of type `string`. This local variable will be used to store and return the concatenated string value.

```
temp.assign(a.s);
temp.len = a.len + b.len;
if (temp.len < max_len)
   strcat(temp.s, b.s);
```

■ The string `a.s` is copied into `temp.s` by calling the `strcpy` library function. The length of the resulting concatenated string is tested to see that it does not exceed the maximum length for strings. If the length is acceptable, the standard library function `strcat` is called with the hidden string members `temp.s` and `b.s`. The references to `temp.s`, `a.s`, and `b.s` are allowed because this function is a `friend` of class `string`.

```
cerr << "Max length exceeded in concatenation.\n";
```

■ The standard error stream `cerr` is used to print an error message, and no concatenation takes place. Only the first string will be returned.

```
return (temp);
```

■ The operator was given a return type of `string`, and `temp` has been assigned the appropriate concatenated string.

1.6 Constructors and Destructors

A constructor is a member function whose job is to initialize a variable of its class. Such a variable is an *object*. In many cases this involves dynamic storage allocation. Constructors are invoked anytime an object of its associated class is created, typically when a variable is declared. A destructor is a member function whose job is to deallocate a variable of its class. Where an object has been allocated dynamically, its associated memory can be deallocated (returned to free store) by a destructor. This is done by implicitly invoking the destructor upon block exit for any class variables declared inside the block.

Let us change our `string` example by dynamically allocating store for each `string` variable. We will replace the private array variable by a pointer. The remodeled class will use a constructor to allocate an appropriate amount of storage dynamically using the `new` operator.

```
//An implementation of dynamically allocated strings.

class string {
   char* s;
   int    len;
public:
   string(int n) { s = new char[n + 1]; len = n; }
   void assign(const char* st) { strcpy(s, st); len = strlen(st); }
   int  length() { return (len); }
   void print() { cout << s << "\nLength: " << len << "\n"; }
   friend string operator + (const string& a, const string& b);
};
```

A constructor is a member function whose name is the same as the class name. The keyword `new` is an addition to the C language. It is a unary operator that takes as an argument a data type that can include an array size. It allocates the appropriate amount of memory to store this type from free store and returns the pointer value that addresses this memory. In the preceding example, n + 1 bytes would be allocated from free store. Thus the declaration

```
string a(40), b(100);
```

would allocate 41 bytes for the variable a, pointed at by a.s , and 101 bytes for the variable b, pointed at by b.s. We add one byte for the end-of-string value 0. Storage obtained by `new` is persistent and is not automatically returned on block exit. When storage return is desired, a destructor function must be included in the class. A destructor is written as an ordinary member function whose name is the same as the class name preceded by the tilde symbol ~ . Typically, a destructor uses the unary operator `delete`, another addition to the language, to automatically deallocate storage associated with a pointer expression.

```
//Add as a member function to class string.
~string() { delete s; } //destructor
```

It is usual to overload the constructor, writing a variety of such functions to accommodate more than one style of initialization. Consider wanting to initialize a string with a pointer to `char` value. Such a constructor is

```
string(const char* p)
{
    len = strlen(p);
    s = new char[len + 1];
    strcpy(s, p);
}
```

A typical declaration invoking this version of the constructor is

```
char*    str = "I came on foot.";
string   a("I came by bus."), b(str);
```

It would also be desirable to have a constructor of no arguments:

```
string() { len = 255; s = new char[255]; }
```

This would be invoked by declarations without parenthesized arguments and would, by default, allocate 255 bytes of memory. Now all three constructors would be invoked in the following declaration:

```
string   a, b(10), c("I came by horse.");
```

The overloaded constructor is selected by the form of each declaration. The variable a has no parameters and so is allocated 255 bytes. The variable b has an integer parameter and so is allocated 11 bytes. The variable c has a pointer parameter to the literal string "I came by horse." and so is allocated 17 bytes, with this literal string copied into its private s member.

1.7 Object-Oriented Programming and Inheritance

The central element of OOP is the encapsulation of an appropriate set of data types and their operations. The class construct with its member functions and data members provides an appropriate coding tool. Class variables are the *objects* to be manipulated.

Classes also provide data hiding. Access privileges can be managed and limited to whatever group of functions needs access to implementation details. This promotes modularity and robustness.

Another important concept in OOP is the promotion of code reuse through the *inheritance* mechanism. This is the mechanism of *deriving* a new class from an existing one called the *base* class. The base class can be added to or altered to create the derived class. In this way a hierarchy of related data types can be created that share code.

Many useful data structures are variants of one another, and it is frequently tedious to produce the same code for each. A derived class inherits the description of the base class. It can then be altered by adding additional members, overloading existing member functions, and modifying access privileges. Without this reuse mechanism, each minor variation would require code replication.

We will imagine that a stockbroker gets in a series of orders that are transactions. There will be different types of transactions. One type will be to buy or sell a stock. A second type will be to buy or sell a call on a stock. A call is an agreement that allows its holder to purchase a stock at an agreed to *strike-price* for a fixed length of time.

In this example we will code a base class `transact`. This class will have information common to subtypes that are derived from it called `stock` and `call`. These types inherit the `public` members of the base class. In OOP the types the user defines correspond to natural parts of the problem domain.

In `transact` there is a `virtual` function `profit_loss`. This function is overloaded in the derived class `stock`. These functions allow for dynamic or run-time typing. A pointer to the base class can also point at objects of the derived classes. When such a pointer is used to point at the overloaded virtual function, it dynamically selects which version of the member function to call. This is a difficult point that will be explained in detail in Chapter 6.

```
//Manipulating transactions using inheritance

#include <iostream.h>

struct transact {        //base class for stock and call
   char     security[20];
   int      p_buy;
   int      p_sell;
   virtual int profit_loss() { return (p_sell - p_buy); }
};

//derived classes
class stock : public transact {
public:
   int  dividend;
   int  profit_loss() { return (dividend + p_sell - p_buy); }
};

class call : public transact {
public:
   int  strike_price;
   int  month;
};

main()
{
   transact* t[2];        //pointers to the base class
   stock     s;
   call      c;

   s.p_buy = 10;
   s.p_sell = 11;
   s.dividend = 2;
   c.p_buy = 10;
   c.p_sell = 11;

   t[0] = &s;             //a base class pointer can
   t[1] = &c;             //point at a derived class

   //the version of profit_loss selected corresponds
   //to the type of the object pointed at
   cout << t[0] -> profit_loss() << "\n";
   cout << t[1] -> profit_loss() << "\n";
}
```

Code reuse is achieved through inheritance. The derived classes `stock` and `call` have their own data members `security[20]`, `p_buy`, and `p_sell` inherited from `transact`. It is easy to modularly extend this code to other transaction categories, such as bonds and puts. Inheritance creates a type hierarchy that can be used dynamically with `virtual` functions.

The OOP programming task is frequently more difficult than normal procedural programming as found in C. There is at least one extra design step before one gets to the coding of algorithms. This involves the hierarchy of types that is useful for the problem at hand. Frequently one is solving the problem more generally than is strictly necessary.

The belief is that this will pay dividends in several ways. The solution will be more encapsulated and thus more robust and easier to maintain and change. Also, the solution will be more reusable. For example, where the code needs a stack, that stack is easily borrowed from existing code. In an ordinary procedural language, such a data structure is frequently "wired into" the algorithm and cannot be exported.

All these benefits are especially important for large coding projects that require coordination among many programmers. Here the ability to have header files specify general interfaces for different classes allows each programmer to work on individual code segments with a high degree of independence and integrity.

1.8 Turbo C++ Considerations

The first thing to do is to take the online interactive tour of the Turbo C++ system provided by *tctour.exe*. This will give you familiarity with basic features of the windowing environment.

Turbo C++ provides an *integrated development environment* (IDE) and a traditional command-line compiler. We will emphasize the IDE, as it is the more useful learning and development tool.

The command-line compiler is invoked as:

tcc prog.cpp

The files appended with *cpp* are compiled as source C++ code into an executable file with a suffix *exe*. The above example if correct ends up as *prog.exe*. The command-line compiler can compile multifile programs and programs that consist of source and object modules that include Turbo C and Turbo C++ code.

The IDE is invoked as:

tc prog.cpp

The integrated environment is brought up on the screen, and its major window is filled with the text of the file *prog.cpp*. In this environment one can edit the file, compile the file, run the resulting executable, display the output, debug the program, and manage a multifile project. Each of these steps is generally considered a part of the program development cycle. IDE integrates these steps conveniently, so as to not require distinct tools for each step in the process. For example, the compiler parses the program and either indicates success or displays in a window a series of error messages. The programmer is then back in the editor and positioned in the source file, so as to conveniently be able to make corrections.

The IDE is best used with a mouse. We will assume that your system has an installed mouse. The alternative is to use keyed commands to obtain the same behavior. The environment is one of multiple movable, resizable windows. The top contains the menu bar, the middle contains the window area, and the bottom contains the status line. The menu bar gives you a list of overall functionality. On this bar are the system menu token (three horizontal lines), *File*, *Edit*, *Run*, *Compile*, *Debug*, *Project*, *Options*, *Window*, and *Help*. By clicking one of its items, a specific menu list appears below the item. For example, clicking on the *File* token gives you a menu of nine choices. Among the choices in the *File* menu are loading a new file, saving the edited text, or exiting the integrated environment. Dragging the mouse and clicking over one of these choices executes that command.

The window area is a rectangle that you can move, zoom, retile, layer, resize, close, and open. At any time you may have one active window and possibly many passive windows. The active window is outlined with a bright double-lined border. The active window is always in the foremost position. Typically one or more windows will contain program text. Commands apply to the active window. For example, if the program text is in the active window, one can click a compile command to compile that code.

A typical window situation is to have an active *Edit* window be the top portion of the screen, below the menu bar, with a smaller *Message* window on the bottom of the screen. The message window displays warning and error messages found while compiling the edit window program. If the code runs, the output is displayed from the DOS environment during execution, and upon program termination the screen redisplays the IDE. During debugging, it is typical to open an *Output* window in order to display DOS command-line text and output. This window is usually tiled in the lower right corner of the screen.

The status line on the bottom of the screen displays both the current actions of the program and hints and shortcuts relevant to the current active window. For example, it might display that the *F1* key gets you on-line help or that *F10* activates the menu bar. You can also click on these commands.

Let us now review a typical edit, compile, debug, and run cycle using the IDE.

1. Invoke the Turbo C++ IDE with the command *tc*. You can now use the menu system provided by the integrated environment. If a mouse is installed, you can drag the mouse and click on the desired menu item. Otherwise you can use the arrow keys to move either left or right across the menu bar and hit the *Enter* key to select an item.

2. We will write a program in a new file *prog.cpp*. Select the *File* command from the menu bar. If not using the mouse, this is easily done by pressing the *Alt* key and the letter *F* key. The *Alt* key plus the first letter of a menu bar item is a shortcut to selecting that item. Select the first option *Open* in the file menu. It will prompt you for a name. Type *prog.cpp* and it will appear in the name box, and click on *Open* or type *Enter*. This creates an edit window. At this point the system automatically places us into this window in the editor.

3. We now select the editor. Initially we will be given an almost blank screen to type in. The screen top will contain the file name and the line and column number. The screen bottom will contain the word `Message`. The bottom part of the screen will be used for error messages. A knowledge of editor commands to insert and modify text is necessary in order to make use of the editor. These commands are explained in Appendix D. The editor is similar to other Borland editors.

4. We compile the program with the command *Run*. This attempts to both compile and run the program. If the compile step detects an error, you are left in the editor with the errors displayed in the *Message* window. Correct the errors and attempt to run the program again.

5. The *Run* executes the compiled program. Any output is displayed on a blank screen. When the program terminates, any key can be hit to return to the edit program for further changes. At this point you can return to the file menu by hitting the *Alt* and *F* key, simultaneously. From there, use menu options to save the file and quit the integrated environment.

After using the integrated environment to write and run a program, we are left with both the file *prog.cpp* and the file *prog.exe*. The latter is executable code. It can now be run either by typing

> *prog*

or by using the full name including the extension tag *exe*

> *prog.exe*

It will be our style to use lowercase for file name and command. The MS-DOS system is case insensitive, and either upper or lowercase can be used for the same command or file name.

If, at another session, you wish to modify an already compiled program, such as *prog.cpp*, the command

> *tc prog.cpp*

will bring up the IDE with this program text ready to be edited. Any recompilation will cause new executable code to be written out to *prog.exe*.

Summary

1. The double slash // is a new comment symbol. The comment runs to the end of the line. The old C bracketing comment symbols /* */ are still available for multiline comments.

2. The *iostream.h* header introduces I/O facilities for C++. The identifier cout is the name of the standard output stream. The operator << passes its argument to standard out. Used in this way, the << is referred to as the *put to* operator.

3. The identifier cin is the name of the standard input stream. The operator >> is the input operator, called *get from*, that assigns values from the input stream to a variable.

4. C++ reduces C's traditional reliance on the preprocessor. Instead of using define, special constants are assigned to variables specified as const. The new keyword inline specifies that a function is to be compiled, if possible, as a macro. As a rule, this should be done sparingly and only on short functions.

5. The syntax of functions in C++ inspired the new function prototype syntax found in ANSI C compilers. Basically, the types of parameters are listed inside the header parentheses, for example, `int add3(int, int, int)`. By explicitly listing the type and number of arguments, strong type checking and assignment-compatible conversions are possible in C++.

6. What is truly novel about C++ is the aggregate type `class`, which is introduced by the language. A `class` is an extension of the idea of `struct` in traditional C. Its use is a way of implementing a data type and associated functions and operators. Therefore a `class` is an implementation of an abstract data type (ADT). There are two important additions to the structure concept: (1) it includes members that are functions, and (2) it employs a new keyword, `public`. This keyword indicates the visibility of the members that follow it. Without this keyword, the members are private to the class. Private members are available for use only by other member functions of the class. Public members are available to any function within the scope of the class declaration. Privacy allows part of the implementation of a class type to be "hidden."

7. The term *overloading* refers to the practice of giving several meanings to an operator or a function. The meaning selected will depend on the types of the arguments used by the operator or function.

8. The keyword `operator` introduces the operator token and replaces what would otherwise be a function name in a function declaration. The keyword `friend` gives a function access to the private members of a class variable. A `friend` function is not a member of the class but has the privileges of a member function in the class in which it is declared.

9. A constructor is a member function whose job is to initialize a variable of its class. In many cases this involves dynamic storage allocation. Constructors are invoked any time an object of its associated class is created, typically when a variable is declared.

10. A destructor is a member function whose job is to deallocate a variable of its class. Where an object has been allocated dynamically, its associated memory can be deallocated (returned to free store) by a destructor. This is done by implicitly invoking the destructor upon block exit for any class variables declared inside the block.

11. The central element of object-oriented programming (OOP) is the encapsulation of an appropriate set of data types and their operations.

These user-defined types are ADTs. The class construct with its member functions and data members provides an appropriate coding tool. Class variables are the *objects* to be manipulated.

12. Another important concept in OOP is the promotion of code reuse through the *inheritance* mechanism. This is the mechanism of *deriving* a new class from an existing one, called the *base* class. The base class can be added to or altered to create the derived class. In this way a hierarchy of related data types can be created that share code. This typing hierarchy can be used dynamically by `virtual` functions. Virtual member functions in a base class are overloaded in a derived class. These functions allow for dynamic or run-time typing. A pointer to the base class can also point at objects of the derived classes. When such a pointer is used to point at the overloaded virtual function, it dynamically selects which version of the member function to call.

Exercises

1. Using stream I/O, write on the screen the words

   ```
   she sells sea shells by the seashore
   ```

   (a) all on one line, (b) on three lines, (c) inside a box.

2. Write a program that will convert distances measured in yards to distances measured in meters. The relationship is 1 meter equals 1.0936 yards. Write the program to use `cin` to read in distances. The program should be a loop that does this calculation until it receives a zero or negative number for input.

3. Most systems allow *redirection* of input/output. In redirection, the symbol < means that input is redirected from the named file, and the symbol > means that output is redirected to the named file. Compile the previous program into an executable *mitok* and execute

   mitok < data > answers

   The file data should contain the numbers:

   1 5 10 26 0

   Print the contents of file *answers* to check the results.

4. Take a working program, omit each line in turn, and run it through the compiler. Record the error messages each such deletion causes. For example, use the following code:

```
#include <iostream.h>

main()
{
    int  m, n, k;
    cout << "\nEnter two integers: ";
    cin  >> m >> n;
    k = m + n;
    cout << "\nTheir sum is " << k << ".\n";
}
```

5. Write a program that asks interactively for your *name* and *age* and responds with

```
Hello name, next year you will be next_age.
```

where *next_age* is *age* + 1 .

6. Write a program that prints out a table of squares, square roots, and cubes. Use either tabbing or strings of blanks to get a neatly aligned table.

```
i     i * i     square root    i * i * i
----------------------------------------------
1          1    1.00000              1
...
```

This topic is covered in detail in Section 7.2.

7. The traditional C swapping function is

```
void swap(i, j)
int*  i;
int*  j;
{
    int  temp;

    temp = *i;
    *i = *j;
    *j = temp;
}
```

Rewrite this using reference parameters and test it.

```
void swap(int& i, int& j)
...
```

8. In traditional C, the following code causes an error:

```
#include <math.h>

main()
{
    printf("%f is the square root of 2.\n", sqrt(2));
}
```

Explain the reason for this and why function prototypes in C++ avoid this problem. Rewrite in C++.

9. Add to the class `string` a member function `reverse`. This function reverses the underlying representation of the character sequence stored in the private member `s`.

10. Add to the class `string` a member function `void print(int k)`. This function overloads `print()` and is meant to print the first `k` characters of the string.

11. Overload the operator `*` in class `string`. Its member declaration will be

```
string operator *(string& a, int n);
```

The `string` represented by `a` should be copied back into `a` `n` times. Check that this does not overrun storage.

12. Using the IDE, rewrite the program in Exercise 6 to also output the fourth root of the integer `i`. This is done by taking the square root of the square root. Open an output window to the right corner of the screen. While debugging the program, use the zoom command found in the window menu to check that the table is properly aligned. To zoom the output window, it is first necessary to make that window active by clicking on its border. The next step is to click the window command on the menu bar, and the last step is to click the zoom option found in that menu.

Chapter 2

C++ as a Better C

C++ extends the C programming language in a number of important ways. Its new features make it more reliable and easier to use than traditional C. Many of these features are independent of the additions connected to the `class` construct. This chapter describes these improvements. Its theme is that C++ can be used as an improved and better C.

Some of the changes described are minor, though useful. Among these is the new comment style. Some of the changes are major, such as function prototypes, which have been adopted into the ANSI C standard. There are also changes in the type compatibility rules. These are stronger in C++, and the compiler provides much of the checking that is relegated to *lint* in traditional C.

Several features of C++ affect type declarations. These include the use of void, void*, enum, and const, all unavailable in traditional C but adopted in more recent compilers and in the ANSI C standard. They also include the use of the keyword inline for function declarations and the use of & to mean the declaration is reference to. All these changes will be explained with examples.

In this chapter, then, we discuss the new comment style, the use of the keywords const and inline, the uses of the void and void* type, the function prototype construct, the use of reference declarations, the overloading of functions, and the use of the free store operators new and delete.

2.1 Comment Style

Programs must be documented to be useful. C++ introduces a one-line comment symbol //. This is in addition to the bracket pair comment symbols /* */ of traditional C. Everything on a single line after the symbol // is treated as a comment. This is even the case when the symbol appears in a string, which is not true for bracket pair comments. The one-line comment symbol is the preferred C++ style. In general it is less error prone—bracket pair symbols can cause problems—for example, when one of the pair is omitted. The following example shows C++ comment style:

```
//The computation of circumference and area of circles.
//                    by
//           Geometrics Inc.
//           Version 2.2

#include <iostream.h>

const  float pi = 3.14159;       //pi accurate to six places
const  int true = 1;             //mnemonic identifier

inline float circum(float rad) { return (pi * 2 * rad); }
inline float area(float rad) { return (pi * rad * rad); }
```

```
main()
{
    float   r;

    while (true) {                      //exit with control-C
        cout << "\nEnter radius: ";     //prompt for input
        cin >> r;
        cout << "\nArea is " << area(r);
        cout << "\nCircumference is " << circum(r) << "\n";
    }
}
```

2.2 Avoiding the Preprocessor: `inline` and `const`

In the previous example and in examples in Chapter 1, the new keywords
`inline` and `const` were used to avoid the use of the preprocessor `define`.
Using the preprocessor to define macros has a clear drawback: namely, the
preprocessor does not understand C syntax. For example:

```
#define SQ(X)   X * X
```

expands the code

```
SQ(a + b)
```

to

```
a + b * a + b
```

This problem is avoided by fully parenthesizing the original macro.
However, the solution does not protect against improper types being used.
This latter defect is remedied by using `inline`.

```
inline int SQ(int x) { return (x * x); }
```

The keyword `inline` is a request to the compiler that the function be compiled as a macro. The compiler may choose to ignore this suggestion, but
either way the semantics are identical. Only very short functions, where
function call overhead is an issue, should use this function specifier.

The `const` keyword is a type specifier. When used alone in a declaration, the base type is implicitly `int`. A variable declared as `const` cannot

have its value changed. Such a variable can be used in places that otherwise would require a literal, such as an array size. A const variable cannot be used on the left-hand side of an assignment, however; thus, unlike a non-const variable, it is not an *lvalue*. An lvalue is an expression that can be used as an address to be stored into. A const variable should also be initialized. As in the previous program, it is used to create named constants, an important documentation aid. Some examples are:

```
const   false = 0;            //implicit type is int
const   double e = 2.71828;   //natural logarithm base
const   int M_size = 100;     //used in an array declaration
const*  p = &M_size;          //a pointer to a constant int
char*   const s = "abcde";    //a constant pointer to char
```

The form

```
const type* identifier
```

declares the identifier as a pointer whose pointed at value is constant. This construct is used where pointer arguments to functions are not to have their contents modified. The form

```
type* const identifier
```

declares the *identifier* as a pointer constant. So,

```
const int* const cp = &M_size;
```

declares cp to be a constant pointer whose pointed at value is constant.

2.3 Declarations

This section describes changes to declarations in C++. It discusses the meaning of enum and illustrates the fact that declarations can be intermixed with executable statements. It also explains that the struct tag name and enum tag name are types.

We shall write a card shuffling program to illustrate these points. First we define a card as a struct.

```
enum suit {clubs, diamonds, hearts, spades};

struct card {
   suit   s;
   int    pips;
};

card deck[52];    //a declaration using card as the type
```

In traditional C, the declaration of deck would be illegal. It would have to be

```
enum suit {clubs, diamonds, hearts, spades};

struct card {
   enum suit   s;
   int         pips;
};

struct card deck[52];
```

In C++, the tag names are types.

Enumerated types were added to C compilers in the early 1980s. Frequently they were implemented with a variety of underlying semantics. C++ treats enumerated types as integer variables, in accord with ANSI C. When listed without initialized values, the identifiers in the enumerated lists are implicitly initialized consecutively starting with 0. These identifiers are named integer constants and may not be changed. So, the two declarations

```
enum suit {clubs, diamonds, hearts, spades};
enum suit {clubs = 0, diamonds = 1, hearts = 2, spades = 3};
```

are equivalent, as are

```
enum suit {clubs = 5, diamonds, hearts, spades = 3};
enum suit {clubs = 5, diamonds = 6, hearts = 7, spades = 3};
```

As we saw in Chapter 1, C++ allows declarations to be intermixed with executable statements. Consider a function that initializes a deck of cards to the normal 52 card values.

```
void init_deck(card d[])
{
    for (int i = 0; i < 52; ++i) {
        d[i].s = (suit)(i / 13);
        d[i].pips = 1 + i % 13;
    }
}
```

In this function the declaration `int i` occurs inside the `for` statement parentheses. The scope of the declaration is the innermost block within which it is found, and the identifier is visible starting at the point at which it is declared. Otherwise the scope rules are the same as in C, which means that declarations can be readily placed near their use.

The program for deck shuffling follows.

```
//  Shuffling a card deck

#include  <iostream.h>
#include  <stdlib.h>            // gets rand, randomize
#include  <time.h>              // used by randomize

enum suit {clubs, diamonds, hearts, spades};

struct card {
    suit   s;
    int    pips;
};

void pr_card(card cd)
{
    switch (cd.pips)  {
        case 1 :  cout << "A"; break;
        case 11:  cout << "J"; break;
        case 12:  cout << "Q"; break;
        case 13:  cout << "K"; break;
        default:  cout << cd.pips;
    }
    switch (cd.s)  {
        case clubs:     cout << "C"; break;
        case diamonds:  cout << "D"; break;
        case hearts:    cout << "H"; break;
        case spades:    cout << "S"; break;
        default :       cerr << "suit error\n"; exit(1);
    }
    cout << "  ";
}
```

```
void init_deck(card d[])
{
    for (int i = 0; i < 52; ++i) {
        d[i].s = (suit)(i / 13);
        d[i].pips = 1 + i % 13;
    }
}
void shuffle(card d[])
{
    for (int i = 0; i < 52; ++i) {
        int k = rand() % 52;        //choose a random card
        card t = d[i];              //swap two cards
        d[i] = d[k];
        d[k] = t;
    }
}

void pr_deck(const card d[])
{
    for (int i = 0; i < 52; ++i) {
        if (i % 13 == 0)
          cout << "\n";
        pr_card(d[i]);
    }
    cout << "\n\n";
}

main()
{
    card deck[52];

    randomize();
    init_deck(deck);
    pr_deck(deck);                  //print unshuffled deck
    shuffle(deck);
    pr_deck(deck);                  //print shuffled deck
}
```

DISSECTION OF THE *shuffle* PROGRAM

```
void shuffle(card d[])
```

■ A function returning no value is of type `void`. The parameter `d` is
of type pointer to `card`.

```
for (int i = 0; i < 52; ++i) {
    int k = rand() % 52;        //choose a random card
    card t = d[i];              //swap two cards
    d[i] = d[k];
    d[k] = t;
}
```

■ Again, there is a mixing of executable statements and declarations. Note how the code is more readable than if the declarations
were at the head of the function block. The `randomize()` function is a Turbo C++ function that uses the system clock to seed
the `rand()` function. The `rand()` function is a pseudorandom
number generator.

2.4 The Uses of `void`

The type `void` was introduced in some C compilers in the early 1980s. It is
standard in ANSI C. In the previous section we saw two of the normal uses
of the keyword `void`. The keyword `void` is used both as the return type of a
function not returning a value and to indicate an empty argument list to a
function. Two additional uses are as a cast and as part of the type pointer to
`void`.

As the type within the cast operator, it informs the compiler that the
expression's computed value is to be discarded.

```
//Simple use of void.

#include <iostream.h>

int foo(int i)
{
    cout << "i is " << i;
    return (i);
}

main()
{
    int k = 5;

    (void)foo(k);   //throw away the int return value
}
```

Most interesting, however, is the use of `void*` as a generic pointer type. This type is also in the ANSI C standard. A pointer declared as type pointer to `void`, as in `void* gp` , can be assigned a pointer value of any underlying base type. But it may not be dereferenced. Dereferencing is the operation `*` acting on a pointer value to obtain what is pointed at. It would not make sense to dereference a pointer to a `void` value. Therefore

```
void* gp;        //generic pointer
int*  ip;        //int pointer
char* cp;        //char pointer

gp = ip;         //legal conversion
ip = gp;         //legal conversion
cp = ip;         //illegal conversion
*ip = 15;        //legal dereferencing of a pointer to int
*ip = *gp;       //illegal dereferencing of a generic pointer
```

A key use for this type is as a formal parameter. For example, the library function `memcpy` is declared in `string.h` as

```
void* memcpy(void* s1, const void* s2, unsigned int n);
```

This function copies n characters from the object based at `s2` into the object based at `s1`. It works with any two pointer types as actual arguments.

2.5 Scope Resolution Operator : :

C is a block-structured language. C++ inherits the same notions of block and scope. In such languages, the same identifier can be used to mean different objects. A use in an inner block *hides* the outer block or external use of the same name. C++ introduces the operator : : called the scope resolution operator. When used in the form : : *variable*, it allows access to the externally named variable. As in the following example, it is assumed that this uncovers an otherwise hidden object. Beware! Because it breaks the modularity of the code, this is a dangerous practice that is rarely justified.

```
//  ::  scope resolution operator

int i = 1;                //external i

#include   <iostream.h>

main()
{
   int   i = 2;           //redeclares i locally

   {
      cout << "enter inner block\n";
      int  n = i;         //the global i is still visible
      int  i = 3;         //hides the global i

      //print the local i and the external i
      cout << i  << "  i <> ::i  " << ::i << "\n";
      cout << "n = " << n << "\n";
   }
   cout << "enter outer block\n";
   cout << i  << "  i <> ::i  " << ::i << "\n";
}
```

The output of this code is

```
enter inner block
3  i <> ::i  1
n = 2
enter outer block
2  i <> ::i  1
```

The major uses of this notation are important for classes. They will be discussed in the following chapters.

2.6 Function Prototypes

The single feature in C++ that most accounts for its greater reliability over traditional C is its use of function prototypes. By explicitly listing the type and number of arguments, strong type checking and assignment-compatible conversions are possible in C++. The success of this feature inspired ANSI C to adopt it.

In traditional C, a function may be declared before it is defined, with the form

type name ( ) ;

This declaration announces that the function is defined elsewhere with the given `return` type. However, the compiler makes no assumptions about type and number of arguments. Therefore, in traditional C, when a function is invoked with an actual argument, the explicit value of that argument is passed as is, without being converted to the defined function's corresponding argument type. A most common error occurs when functions such as `sqrt` are passed `int` valued expressions.

```
printf("%f is sqrt of 4\n", sqrt(4));
```

This prints 0 on many traditional C systems. The function `sqrt` expects a `double`, and the bit configuration for the `int` constant 4, when interpreted as `double`, passes `sqrt` an argument whose value is 0.

In C++ the prototype form is

type name (*argument-declaration-list*) ;

Examples are:

```
double sqrt(double x);
void   make_str(char*, int);      //definition has names
void   print(const char* s);      //s is not modified
int    printf(char* format, ...); //variable no. of args
```

With the above `sqrt` prototype definition, the call to

```
sqrt(4)
```

causes a conversion from `int` value 4 to `double` value 4 to occur before the function call is executed. The argument-declaration-list can either have named arguments or omit them. These names are intended as possible documentation. It is not necessary, but it is good style for names in prototype declarations to match names used in the actual definition. The prototype for the `stdio.h` function `printf` has an ellipsis "..." that is used to specify that the function argument list has unknown length and type.

The following example illustrates these points.

```
//Compute the average of a set of int values.

#include <iostream.h>

int data[10] = {99, 87, 67, 90, 66, 43, 89, 88, 97, 76};

main()
{
    void   pr_arr(const char*, const int*, int);
    void   pr_dbl(const char* name, double x);
    double avg_arr(const int a[], int size);

    pr_arr("data", data, 10);
    pr_dbl("average", avg_arr(data, 10));
}

void pr_int(const char* name, int k)
{
    cout << name << " = " << k << "\n";
}

void pr_dbl(const char* name, double x)
{
    cout << name << " = " << x << "\n";
}

void pr_arr(const char* name, const int a[], int size)
{
    cout << name ;
    pr_int(" array, size ", size);
    for (int i = 0; i < size; ++i)
       cout << a[i] << "\t";
    cout << "\n";
}
```

```
double avg_arr(const int a[], int size)    //compute average
{
    int   sum = 0;

    for (int i = 0; i < size; ++i)
        sum += a[i];
    return ((double) sum / size);
}
```

The output from this program is

```
data array, size  = 10
99     87     67     90     66     43     89     88     97     76
average = 80.2
```

2.7 Call-by-Reference and Reference Declarations

C++ allows *reference to* declarations. These are typically of the form

>   *type& identifier = object*

Such declarations declare the identifier to be an alternative name for an object specified in an initialization of the reference. Some examples are:

```
int     n;
int&    nn = n;         //nn is an alternative name for n
double  a[10];
double& last = a[9];    //last is an alias for a[9]
char&   new_line = '\n';
```

In these examples, the names n and nn are aliases for each other; that is, they refer to the same object. Modifying nn is equivalent to modifying n, and vice versa. The name last is an alternative to the single array element a[9]. These names, once initialized, cannot be changed. Also, it is possible to initialize a reference to a literal. In the examples, new_line is initialized to the char constant \n, which creates a reference to the otherwise unknown location where the literal is stored.

The chief use of reference declarations is in formal parameter lists. This usage allows C++ to have *call-by-reference* arguments directly. Let us use this mechanism to write a function greater that exchanges two values if the first is greater than the second.

```
int greater(int& a, int& b)
{
   if (a > b) {       //exchange
      int temp = a;
      a = b;
      b = temp;
      return (1);
   }
   else
      return (0);
}
```

Now, if i and j are two int variables, then

```
greater(i, j)
```

will use the reference to i and the reference to j to exchange, if necessary, their two values. In traditional C, this operation must be accomplished using pointers and dereferencing.

2.8 Default Arguments

A formal parameter can be given a default argument. This is usually a constant that occurs frequently when the function is called. Use of a default argument saves writing in this default value at each invocation. The following function illustrates the point.

```
int mult(int n, int k = 2)     //k = 2 is default
{
   if (k == 2)
      return (n * n);
   else
      return (mult(n, k - 1) * n);
}
```

We assume that most of the time the function is used to return the value of n squared.

```
mult(i + 5)                 //computes (i + 5) * (i + 5)
mult(i + 5, 3)              //computes (i + 5) cubed
```

Only the trailing parameters of a function can have default values. Some examples are

```
void foo(int i, int j = 7);                //legal
void goo(int i = 3, int j);                //illegal
void hoo(int i, int j = 3, int k = 7);     //legal
void moo(int i = 1, int j = 2, int k = 3); //legal
void noo(int i, int j = 2, int k);         //illegal
```

2.9 Overloading Functions

The term *overloading* refers to using the same name for multiple meanings of an operator or a function. The meaning selected depends on the types of the arguments used by the operator or function. Here we restrict our discussion to function overloading and leave operator overloading to later chapters, as the latter is chiefly used in the context of classes.

The usual reason for picking a function name is to indicate the function's chief purpose. Readable programs generally have a diverse and literate choice of identifiers. Sometimes different functions are used for the same purpose. For example, consider a function that averages the values in an array of double versus one that averages the values in an array of int. Both are conveniently named avg_arr, as in a previous example.

```
double avg_arr(const double a[], int size);
double avg_arr(const int a[], int size);

double avg_arr(const int a[], int size)
{
    int   sum = 0;

    for (int i = 0; i < size; ++i)
        sum += a[i];        //performs int arithmetic
    return ((double) sum / size);
}

double avg_arr(const double a[], int size)
{
    double  sum = 0.0;

    for (int i = 0; i < size; ++i)
        sum += a[i];        //performs double arithmetic
    return (sum / size);
}
```

The following code shows how each is invoked:

```
main()
{
   int    w[5] = {1, 2, 3, 4, 5};
   double x[5] = {1.1, 2.2, 3.3, 4.4, 5.5};

   cout << avg_arr(w, 5) << "  int array average\n";
   cout << avg_arr(x, 5) << "  double array average\n";
}
```

The compiler chooses the function with matching types and arguments.

2.10 Free Store Operators `new` **and** `delete`

The unary operators `new` and `delete` are available to manipulate *free store*. They are more convenient than and can be used to replace the standard library functions `malloc`, `calloc`, and `free` in many applications. Free store is a system-provided memory pool for objects whose lifetime is directly managed by the programmer. The programmer creates the object by using `new` and destroys the object by using `delete`. This is important for dynamic data structures such as lists and trees.

The operator `new` is used in the following forms:

```
new type-name
new type-name initializer
new (type-name)
```

In each case there are minimally two effects. First, an appropriate amount of store is allocated from free store to contain the named type. Second, the base address of the object is returned as the value of the `new` expression. The expression is of type `void*` and can be assigned to any pointer type variable. The operator `new` returns the value 0 when memory is unavailable.

The following example uses `new`:

```
int* ptr_i;
ptr_i = new int(5);    //allocation and initialization
```

In this code, the pointer to `int` variable `ptr_i` is assigned the address of the store obtained in allocating an object of type `int`. The location pointed at by `ptr_i` is initialized to the value 5. This use is not usual for a simple type such as `int`, in that it is far more convenient and natural to automatically allocate an integer variable on the stack or globally.

The operator `delete` destroys an object created by `new`, in effect returning its allocated storage to free store for reuse. The following example uses these constructs to dynamically allocate an array:

```
//Use of new operator to dynamically allocate an array.

#include <iostream.h>

main()
{
    int*   data;
    int    size;

    cout << "\nEnter array size: ";
    cin >> size;

    data = new int[size];
    for (int j = 0; j < size; ++j)
        cout << (data[j] = j) << "\t";
    cout << "\n\n";

    delete data;
    data = new int[size];
    for (j = 0; j < size; ++j)
        cout << data[j] << "\t";
}
```

DISSECTION OF THE *dynamic* PROGRAM

```
int*   data;
int    size;

cout << "\nEnter array size: ";
cin >> size;

data = new int[size];
```

■ The pointer variable `data` is used as the base address of a dynamically allocated array whose number of elements is the value of `size`. The user is prompted for the integer-valued `size`. The `new` operator is used to allocate storage from free store capable of storing an object of type `int[size]`. On a system such as Turbo C++ where integers take 2 bytes, this would allocate 2 * `size` bytes. At this point `data` is assigned the base address of this store.

```
for (int j = 0; j < size; ++j)
   cout << (data[j] = j) << "\t";
```

■ This statement initializes the values of the `data` array and prints them.

```
delete data;
```

■ The operator `delete` returns the storage associated with the pointer variable `data` to free store. This can be done only with objects allocated by `new`.

```
data = new int[size];
for (j = 0; j < size; ++j)
   cout << data[j] << "\t";
```

■ We access free store again, but this time we do not initialize the `data` array. On a typical system, the same memory just returned to free store is used, with the old values reappearing. However, there are no guarantees on what values will appear in objects allocated from free store. Test this on your system. The programmer is responsible for properly initializing such objects.

The operator `delete` is used in the following forms:

```
delete expression
delete [ expression ] expression
```

The first form is the most common. The expression is typically a pointer variable used in a previous `new` expression. The second form is occasionally used when returning store that was allocated as an array type. The bracketed expression gives the number of elements of the array. The operator `delete` does not return a value. Equivalently, one can say its return type is `void`.

2.11 Odds and Ends

Several other features of C++ that do not appear in traditional C are relatively minor. Among these are the use of `signed`, the treatment of `float`, and the use of anonymous unions. We shall treat these matters briefly.

The ANSI C standard introduces the keyword `signed`, which is analogous to the keyword `unsigned`. The keywords `signed` and `unsigned` are type specifiers for the integral types. The `unsigned` type does not allow negative values; the `signed` type does.

The type `float` in traditional C was always promoted to `double` when used in expressions. C++, however, reserves the right to do arithmetic in single precision `float`.

An anonymous `union` is a `union` declared without a tag name. C++ allows the member names of such unions to be used directly, but they must be distinct from other identifiers defined within the same scope. A global anonymous union has to have storage class `static`. An example is:

```
//Anonymous Unions

#include <iostream.h>

static union {
    long int    i;
    char        c[4];
    float       w;
};

main()
{
    i = 65;
    cout << c[0] << "\n";
    c[1] = c[2] = c[3] = 'A';
    cout << w << "\n";
}
```

What gets printed is

```
A
12.078431
```

The byte that is used by the integer member i to store the value 65 is accessed by the indexed character member c[0]. The string of four A's stored in the array c[] is interpreted by Turbo C++ as the floating point value 12.07841. This code is highly machine dependent. In a union the member declarations share the same storage. This technique is used to conserve storage and avoid unnecessary type conversions.

2.12 Turbo C++ Considerations

We shall use the *union.cpp* program to describe a number of Turbo C++ features. How values are represented for the basic types in C and C++ is found in *limits.h* and *float.h*. How this program was converted and debugged from an earlier version found in *C++ for C Programmers* by Ira Pohl (Benjamin/Cummings, Redwood City, California, 1989) is explained. We shall illustrate the use of the IDE to find and correct syntax errors and run-time behavior.

Arithmetic Types

C has built-in types ranging in size from char to long double. The char type stores ASCII characters (see Appendix A) or alternatively can be thought of as a one-byte integer type capable of storing values from –128 to 127. At the other extreme, a Turbo C++ long double is stored in 10 bytes and has an exponent range from –4932 to 4932 in base 10. It is capable of manipulating floating point numbers with 19-digit precision.

The integer types are stored as 2's complement numbers with the lead bit or most significant bit being the sign bit. The standard int type is two bytes and is capable of storing values from –32,768 to 32,767. The long type is four bytes and is capable of storing values from –2,147,483,648 to 2,147,483,647. The enum types are stored as int. An enum declaration creates a distinct type that is not assignment compatible with other enumeration types.

The floating types are, in order of size, *float*, *double*, and *long double*, occupying four, eight, and ten bytes, respectively. They are stored with the most significant bit being the sign bit, followed by an exponent part, and finally by a fraction part (also known as the significand or mantissa). Some relevant definitions as found in *float.h* are:

```
#define FLT_DIG                6
#define DBL_DIG                15
#define LDBL_DIG               19

#define FLT_MANT_DIG           24
#define DBL_MANT_DIG           53
#define LDBL_MANT_DIG          64

#define FLT_MAX_10_EXP         +38
#define DBL_MAX_10_EXP         +308
#define DBL_MAX_10_EXP         +4932

#define FLT_EPSILON            1.19209290E-07F
#define DBL_EPSILON            2.2204460492503131E-16
#define LDBL_EPSILON           1.084202172485504E-19
```

Using `float` as an example, we have for Turbo C++ that `FLT_DIG` means 6 decimal digit precision, `FLT_MANT_DIG` means 24 bits used to represent the fraction, `FLT_MAX_10_EXP` means 10 to the 38th is the largest exponent, and `FLT_EPSILON` means `1.19209290E-07F` is the smallest difference between two `float` values.

In *union.cpp* the array element `c[0]` would overlap the least significant byte of the integer value 65. Thus an `A` is printed using `c[0]`. Storing four `A`'s in the character array `c[]` and using `w` to output a `float` value prints `12.07841`.

Syntax Errors

The original form of *union.cpp* used AT&T C++ version 1.2 running on a SUN. It was in file *union.c*:

```
//Anonymous Unions

#include <stream.h>

union {
    int     i;
    char    c[4];
    double  w;
};

main()
{
    i = 65;
    cout << form("%c", c[3]) << "\n";
}
```

We use the IDE editor to convert *stream.h* to the newer I/O package *iostream.h* and then execute the compile command. What gets printed in the message window below the edit window named *union.c* are a large number of error messages. It turns out that we forget to use the *cpp* suffix. Renaming the file to *union.cpp* and compiling leaves two error messages:

```
Error D:\DEB\UNION.CPP 7: Global anonymous union not static
Error D:\DEB\UNION.CPP 12: Function 'form' should have a prototype
                          in function main
```

These syntax errors include file and line number information. Clicking on them gets us into the edit window ready to correct the error. We correct the first error by adding `static` to the union declaration. This is a change in how release 2.0 requires anonymous unions to be linked. We also realize that `form()` is a holdover from old stream I/O. We edit that line to read:

```
   cout <<   c[3] << "\n";
```

and click on the compile command.

The compiler has compiled successfully and now we wish to run the program. We go to the window menu and click on the *Output* token. This gets us a window from which to watch program output. We use the window menu *Tile* command to reposition all the active windows so that they are not obscuring each other. We click on the run menu and select the run option. Running the program shows a garbage character appearing on the screen instead of the expected `A`. We can switch the screen back and forth to the full output screen by hitting *Alt-F5*.

We are puzzled and decide to inspect the character array while executing the program. We choose the *Inspect* option from the debug menu. A *Dialog* box appears prompting us for a variable name. We type `c` and click *Okay* and an inspection box appears. We place the cursor in the edit window following the line `i = 65;` and use the *Go To Cursor* command. This runs the program up to that point. The inspection window now has four array elements with `c[0]` having contents `A`. Our mistake was to forget that the program had originally been developed on a machine architecture where the 4 bytes stored characters in the reverse order from our Turbo C++ system. We modify our program to print `c[0]` and it now runs correctly.

Turbo C++ provides a comprehensive set of debugging aids. The IDE integrates the entire edit, compile, run, and debug cycle.

Summary

1. Programs must be documented to be useful. C++ introduces a one-line comment symbol `//`. This is in addition to the bracket pair comment symbols `/* */` of traditional C. Everything on a single line after the symbol `//` is treated as a comment.

2. The keyword `inline` is a request to the compiler that the function be compiled as a macro. Only very short functions, where function call overhead is an issue, should use this function specifier. The `const` keyword is a type specifier. When used alone in a declaration, the base type is implicitly `int`. A variable declared as `const` cannot have its value changed. It can be used in places that otherwise would require a literal, such as an array size. It cannot be used on the left-hand side of an assignment; thus, unlike a non-`const` variable, it is not an *lvalue*.

3. Enumerated types were added to C compilers in the early 1980s. C++ treats them as integer variables in accord with ANSI C. When listed without initialized values, the identifiers in the enumerated lists are implicitly initialized consecutively starting with 0. These identifiers are named integer constants and may not be changed.

4. The tag names of both enumerated and structure types can be used as type names. Declarations may be intermixed with executable statements.

5. The type `void` was introduced in some C compilers in the early 1980s. It is standard in ANSI C. It improves both documentation and type checking over traditional C. The keyword `void` is used as the return type of a function not returning a value. Three further uses are as a cast, as part of the type pointer to `void`, or optionally as an empty argument list.

6. C++ introduces the operator `::` called the scope resolution operator. When used in the form `::` *variable*, it allows access to the externally named variable.

7. The single feature in C++ that most accounts for its greater reliability over traditional C is its use of function prototypes. By explicitly listing the type and number of arguments, strong type checking and assignment-compatible conversions are possible in C++. In C++ the prototype form is:

    type name (*argument-declaration-list*) ;

Examples are:

```
double sqrt(double x);
void   make_str(char*, int);      //definition has names
void   print(const char* s);      //s is not modified
int    printf(char* format, ...); //variable no. of args.
```

8. C++ allows *reference to* declarations. These are typically of the form

    type & *identifier* = *object*

   These declare the identifier to be an alternative name for an object specified in an initialization of the reference. The chief use of reference declarations is in formal parameter lists. This allows C++ to have *call-by-reference* arguments.

9. A formal parameter can be given a default argument. This is usually a constant that occurs frequently when the function is called. Use of the default argument saves writing in this default value at each invocation.

10. The term *overloading* refers to using the same name for various meanings of an operator or a function. The meaning selected depends on the types of the arguments used by the operator or function. C++ introduces the keyword `overload` to indicate that a particular name will be so used. This keyword is a function specifier and is used only in declarations of type function.

11. The unary operators `new` and `delete` are available to manipulate *free store*. Free store is a system-provided memory pool for objects whose lifetime is directly managed by the programmer. The programmer creates the object by using `new` and destroys the object by using `delete`. The operator `new` is used in the following forms:

    `new` *type-name*
    `new` *type-name initializer*
    `new` (*type-name*)

   The expression is of type `void*` and can be assigned to any pointer type variable.

Exercises

1. C++ style follows C style in layout. Generally a tab stop of three to five blank spaces is used to indent sections of code to reflect flow of control. Proper commenting and choice of identifier names are important to readable code. Try to understand the following code and rewrite it in good style:

```
#include <iostream.h>
const float f = 3.14159;
inline float v(float b) {return 4*f*b*b*b/3.0; }
main() {float b; while (1) { cout << "enter b"; cin >> b;
cout << "\nVolume is " << v(b) << "\n"; }}
```

2. Can you have the following as comments in C and C++?

```
//one liner
/*one liner
/*   old style  */
/*   is nesting /* allowed */ on your system? */
//what happens if we repeat // on this line
a /*p; where p is a pointer
"/* within a string */"
"// within a string"
//  /* within a one liner */
/*  //okay I give up  */
```

3. Recode the following #define preprocessor lines using const and inline declarations:

```
#define TRUE          1
#define c             299792.4562  //light speed in km/sec
#define EOF           (-1)
#define LARGER(X,Y)   ((X > Y) ? (X) : (Y))
#define CUBE(X)       (X) * (X) * (X)
```

4. Using the declaration of card deck[52] as found in this chapter, write code that will deal out and print 6 five-card hands. A hand should be stored in a two-dimensional array:

```
const int players = 6;
const int nc       = 5;
card  hand[players][nc];
```

5. Continuing with Exercise 4, write code that checks if a hand is a flush. A flush is a hand that contains five or more cards of the same suit. It can be tested by summing for each suit the number of cards of that suit that occur. You will write the function

    ```
    int is_flush(card h[]);   //returns 1 if a flush else 0
    ```

    Generate 1000 deals at random, and print out the probability of getting a flush.

6. On most C compilers the following program runs:

    ```
    char strg[5] = "ABCD";

    main()
    {
        int  i = 7, *p = &i;
        char* c;

        c = *p;
        c = strg + 1;
        *c = 'X';
    }
    ```

    On C++ compilers the program gives a syntax error. Discuss these differences. Which is preferred?

7. The following program uses pointer types and modifies a string:

    ```
    #include <iostream.h>

    main()
    {
        char*  c;
        char*  const strg = "ABCD";

        cout << "\nstrg is " << strg;
        c = strg + 1;
        *c = 'X';
        cout << "\n strg is " <<  strg;
    }
    ```

    What is wrong with changing the strg declaration to

    ```
    const char*  const strg = "ABCD";
    ```

8. Given the following declarations:

```
int    i = 5;
int*   pi = &i;
char   c = 'C';
char*  pc = &c;
void*  pv;
char   s[100];
```

what do the following expressions mean? Are any illegal under C++ typing?

```
*pi = i + c;
*pc = s + 10;
pc  = s + 10;
pv  = pi;
pv  = s + 1;
pv  = ++s;
pc  = pv;
*pc = *pv;
*pc = (char)*pv;
```

9. Use the library function `memcpy` to copy a string into another character array. Also copy an integer array into another integer array. Finally, copy a character array into an integer array. On most systems the header `string.h` has `memcpy`.

10. Implement your own version of `memcpy` to conform to the function prototype found in Section 2.4.

11. What gets printed by the following code?

```
//  ::  scope resolution operator

double x = 1.23;

#include  <iostream.h>

main()
{
   double   x = 2.34;

   {
       double  y = x;
       double  x = 3.45;
       cout << x  << "  x <> ::x   " << ::x << "\n";
       cout << "y = " << y << "\n";
   }
   cout << x  << "  x <> ::x   " << ::x << "\n";
}
```

12. The following traditional C function uses pointer variables and dereferencing to implement a circular shift:

```
void shift(pc1, pc2, pc3, pc4)
char*   pc1;
char*   pc2;
char*   pc3;
char*   pc4;
{
    char   temp;

    temp = *pc1;
    *pc1 = *pc2;
    *pc2 = *pc3;
    *pc3 = *pc4;
    *pc4 = temp;
}
```

Convert it to a function in C++ using call-by-reference.

```
void shift(char& c1, char& c2, char& c3, char& c4) . . .
```

Write a test program that prints the before and after values using shift.

13. The following function computes the minimum and maximum values found in an array:

```
//Find both the minimum and maximum values of an array.

void minmax(const int data[], int size, int* min, int* max)
{
    *min = *max = data[0];
    for (int i = 1; i < size; ++i)
        if (*min > data[i])
            *min = data[i];
        else if (*max < data[i])
            *max = data[i];
}
```

Convert it to a function that uses call-by-reference. Write a program to test it.

14. A more efficient method for finding minimum and maximum is as follows. Compare a pair of elements and use the smaller element for finding the minimum and the larger element for finding the maximum. With this method, rewrite the function used in Exercise 13. How many com-

parisons are saved over the previous method? A description of this
method is found in A Sorting Method and Its Complexity, *Communica-
tions of the ACM*, vol. 15, no. 6, 1972, by Ira Pohl.

15. Change the solution to Exercise 13 to use a default `size` parameter. Let
the default value be 10. (Reminder: The argument `size` must now be at
the end of the argument list.)

16. Write three overloaded functions that each print an array. One will print
an array of `int`, the second an array of `float`, and the third an array of
`char`.

```
void print(const int data[], int size = 20);    //int version
void print(const float data[], int size = 20); //float version
void print(const char data[], int size = 20);   //char version
```

Note that each declaration has a default value for `size`. Use stream I/O
when writing each function.

17. First write a function that creates a vector of a user-keyed `size` and
that reads in, using `cin`, its size and initial values.

```
void create_vec(int* &v, int& size);
//get array size from cin
//use new to create v[size]
//and then use a for loop to assign values from cin
```

Next write a function that will add two vectors. If the vectors are not
the same size, add them for the lesser of the two sizes.

```
void add_vec(const int* v1, const int* v2, int* sum, int size);
//add_vec  returns vector sum   sum[i] = v1[i] + v2[i]
```

Finally, print out the resulting array:

```
void print_vec (const int* v, int size);
```

18. The following code uses `new` to allocate a two-dimensional array:

```
//Dynamically allocated two dimensional arrays
#include <iostream.h>

main()
{
    int**  data;
    int    sz1, sz2, i, j;
```

```
        cout << "\nEnter two sizes: ";
        cin >> sz1 >> sz2;
        data = new int* [sz1];          //an array of pointers
        for (i = 0; i < sz1; ++i)
           data[i] = new int[sz2];      //each row is allocated
        cout << "\nEnter " << sz1 << " by " << sz2 << " ints\n";
        for (i = 0; i < sz1; ++i)
           for (j = 0; j < sz2; ++j)
              cin >> data[i][j];
        for (i = 0; i < sz1; ++i)
           for (j = 0; j < sz2; ++j)
              cout << data[i][j] << "\t";
        cout << "\n";
     }
```

Notice that you must do the allocation in two stages. This is because C has a simple linear interpretation of an array. Use the ideas found in this code to write two-dimensional routines, `create_matrix` and `add_matrix`. These are analogous to the functions written in Exercise 17.

19. Anonymous unions must be used carefully, as they are machine dependent. Let us use them to check on conversion between the types `long int` and `float`. Fill in the *Prints* column in the following table.

Declarations and assignments		

```//external to main```
 ```union {```
 ``` long int j;```
 ``` float   y;```
 ```};```
 ```//in main```
 ```long int   i = 1024;```
 ```float x = 1.0;```		

Expression	Output expression	Prints
j = i	cout << j	1024
j = i	cout << y	
y = x	cout << j	
y = 2 * x	cout << y	

Chapter 3

Classes

This chapter introduces the reader to `struct` and `class`. The original name given by Stroustrup to his language was "C with classes." A `class` is an extension of the idea of `struct` found in traditional C. It is a way of implementing a data type and associated functions and operators. User-defined data types, such as stack, complex numbers, and card decks, are examples of ADT implementation. Each of these types is coded in C++ and used in a major example in this chapter.

We shall explain here the new concept of `class` by first reviewing how traditional C structures work. In C++, structures may have member functions. Structures also can have parts of their description `private`. Both of

63

these extensions will be described here. These extensions lead naturally to the `class` concept that, in effect, is a `struct` with a default visibility of `private`.

Allowing private and public visibility for members gives the programmer control over what parts of the data structure are modifiable. The private parts are hidden from client code, and the public parts are available. It is possible to change the hidden representation but not to change the public access or functionality. If done properly, client code need not change when the hidden representation is modified. A large part of the OOP design process involves thinking up the appropriate ADTs for a problem. Good ADTs not only model key features of the problem but also are frequently reusable in other code.

3.1 The Aggregate Type `struct`

The structure type allows the programmer to aggregate components into a single named variable. A structure has components, called *members*, that are individually named. Since the members of a structure can be of various types, the programmer can create aggregates that are suitable for describing complicated data.

As a simple example, let us define a structure that will describe a playing card. The spots on a card that represent its numeric value are called *pips*. A playing card, such as the three of spades, has a pip value, 3, and a suit value, spades. As in Chapter 2, we can declare the structure type:

```
enum suit {clubs, diamonds, hearts, spades};

struct card {
   suit  s;
   int   pips;
};
```

In traditional C, the declaration of `card` would be illegal. It would have to be

```
struct card {
   enum suit  s;
   int        pips;
};
```

As we described in Chapter 2, in C++, the tag names are types. Our examples will use this C++ innovation. In this declaration, `struct` is a keyword, `card` is the structure tag name, and the variables `pips` and `suit` are members of the structure. The variable `pips` will take values from 1 to 13, representing ace to king.

This declaration creates the derived data type `struct card`, or in C++ the type `card`. The declaration can be thought of as a template; it creates the type, but no storage is allocated. The declaration

```
card    c1, c2;
```

allocates storage for the identifiers `c1` and `c2`, which are of type `card`. To access the members of `c1` and `c2`, we use the structure member operator " . ". Suppose we want to assign to `c1` the values representing the five of diamonds and to `c2` the values representing the queen of spades. To do this we can write

```
c1.pips = 5;
c1.suit = diamonds;
c2.pips = 12;
c2.suit = spades;
```

A construct of the form

structure_variable . member_name

is used as a variable in the same way a simple variable or an element of an array is used. The member name must be unique within the specified structure. Since the member must always be prefaced or accessed through a unique structure variable identifier, there is no confusion between two members having the same name in different structures. An example is

```
struct fruit {
    char    name[15];
    int     calories;
};

struct vegetable {
    char    name[15];
    int     calories;
};
```

```
fruit        a;      //struct fruit      a; in traditional C
vegetable    b;      //struct vegetable b; in traditional C
```

Having made these declarations, we can access a.calories and b.calories without ambiguity.

3.2 Structure Pointer Operator

We have already seen the use of the member operator " . " in accessing members. In this section we introduce the structure pointer operator -> .

C provides the structure pointer operator -> to access the members of a structure via a pointer. This operator is typed on the keyboard as a *minus* sign followed by a *greater than* sign. If a pointer variable is assigned the address of a structure, then a member of the structure can be accessed by a construct of the form

pointer_to_structure -> *member_name*

An equivalent construct is given by

(**pointer_to_structure*) . *member_name*

The operators -> and " . ", along with () and [], have the highest precedence, and they associate *left to right*. In complicated situations the two accessing modes can be combined. The following table illustrates their use in a straightforward manner.

Declarations and assignments		

`card cd, *p = &cd;`
`card deck[52];`
 	
`cd.pips = 5;`
`cd.s = spades;`
`deck[0] = cd;`		

Expression	**Equivalent expression**	**Value**
cd.pips	p -> pips	5
cd.suit	p -> suit	spades
deck[0].pips	deck -> pips	5
(*p).suit	p -> suit	spades

3.3 An Example: Stack

The stack is one of the most useful standard data structures.

A stack is a data structure that allows insertion and deletion of data to occur only at a single restricted element, the top of the stack. This is the last-in-first-out discipline (LIFO). Conceptually, it behaves like a pile of trays that pops up or is pushed down when trays are removed or added. Typically, a stack allows as operations *push*, *pop*, *top*, *empty*, and *full*. The push operator places a value on the stack. The pop operator retrieves and deletes a value off the stack. The top operator returns the top value from the stack. The empty operator tests if the stack is empty. The full operator tests if the stack is full. The stack is a typical ADT.

We wish to implement a stack as a C++ data type using `struct` in its traditional form. An implementation choice will be to use a fixed-length `char` array to store the contents of the stack. The top of the stack will be an integer-valued member named `top`. The various stack operations will be implemented as functions, each of whose argument lists includes a pointer to `stack` parameter. This will avoid copying a potentially large stack to perform a simple operation.

```
//A traditional C implementation of type stack.

const int max_len = 1000;
enum boolean {false, true};
enum {EMPTY = -1, FULL = max_len - 1};

struct stack {
   char s[max_len];
   int  top;
};

void reset(stack* stk)
{
   stk -> top = EMPTY;
}

void push(char c, stack* stk)
{
   stk -> top++;
   stk -> s[stk -> top] = c;
}
```

```
char pop(stack* stk)
{
    return (stk -> s[stk -> top--]);
}

char top(stack* stk)
{
    return (stk -> s[stk -> top]);
}

boolean empty(const stack* stk)
{
    return (boolean)(stk -> top == EMPTY);
}

boolean full(const stack* stk)
{
    return (boolean)(stk -> top == FULL);
}
```

DISSECTION OF THE *stack* FUNCTIONS

```
const int max_len = 1000;
enum boolean {false, true};
enum {EMPTY = -1, FULL = max_len - 1};

struct stack {
    char s[max_len];
    int  top;
};
```

■ We declare a new type `boolean`. In C++ the tag name of an
  `enum` type is a new type. The constant `false` is initialized to 0,
  and the constant `true` is initialized to 1. The `struct` declaration
  creates the new type `stack`. It has two members, the array member `s` and the `int` member `top`.

```
void reset(stack* stk)
{
    stk -> top = EMPTY;
}
```

■ This function is used for initialization. The member `top` is assigned the value `EMPTY`. The stack starts out as empty. The particular stack that this works on is an argument passed in as an address.

```
void push(char c, stack* stk)
{
    stk -> top++;
    stk -> s[stk -> top] = c;
}
char pop(stack* stk)
{
    return (stk -> s[stk -> top--]);
}
```

■ The operation *push* is implemented as a function of two arguments. The member `top` is incremented. The value of `c` is shoved onto the top of the stack. This function assumes that the stack is not full. The operation *pop* is implemented in like fashion. It assumes the stack is not empty. The value of the top of the stack is returned, and the member `top` is decremented.

```
boolean empty(const stack* stk)
{
    return (boolean)(stk -> top == EMPTY);
}
boolean full(const stack* stk)
{
    return (boolean)(stk -> top == FULL);
}
```

■ These functions return an enumerated type `boolean` value. Each tests the `stack` member `top` for an appropriate condition. In all functions the stack argument is passed in as address, and the structure pointer operator `->` is used to access members.

Given that these declarations reside in the file `stack.h`, we can test these operations with the following program, which enters the characters of a string onto a stack and pops them, printing each character out in reverse order:

```
//Test of stack implementation by reversing a string.

#include <iostream.h>
#include "stack.h"       //stack implementation imported

main()
{
    stack  s;
    char   str[40] = {"My name is Betty Dolsberry!"};
    int    i = 0;

    cout << str << "\n";       //print the string
    reset(&s);
    while (str[i])             //push onto stack
        if (!full(&s))
            push(str[i++], &s);
    while (!empty(&s))         //print the reverse
        cout << pop(&s);
    cout << "\n";
}
```

The output from this test program is

```
My name is Betty Dolsberry!
!yrrebsloD ytteB si eman yM
```

Note that one of the actual arguments to each function is `&s`, the address of the stack variable declared in `main`. This argument is given because each function expects an address of a `stack` variable.

3.4 Member Functions

The concept of `struct` is augmented in C++ to allow functions to be members. The function declaration is included in the structure declaration and is invoked by using access methods for structure members. The idea is that the functionality required by the `struct` data type should be directly included in the `struct` declaration. This construct improves the encapsulation of the ADT stack operations by packaging it directly with its data representation.

Let us rewrite our stack example by declaring as member functions the various functions associated with the stack:

```
struct stack {
    //data representation

    char s[max_len];
    int  top;
    enum {EMPTY = -1, FULL = max_len - 1};

    //operations represented as member functions

    void    reset() { top = EMPTY; }
    void    push(char c) { top++; s[top] = c; }
    char    pop() { return (s[top--]); }
    char    top_of() { return (s[top]); }
    boolean empty() { return (boolean)(top == EMPTY); }
    boolean full() { return (boolean)(top == FULL); }
};
```

The member functions are written much as other functions. One difference is that they can use the data member names as is. Thus the member functions in `stack` use `top` and `s` in an unqualified manner. When invoked on a particular object of type `stack`, they act on the specified member in that object.

The following example illustrates these ideas. If two `stack` variables

```
stack data, operands;
```

are declared, then

```
data.reset();
operands.reset();
```

invoke the member function `reset`, which has the effect of setting both `data.top` and `operands.top` to `EMPTY`. If a pointer to `stack`

```
stack* ptr_operands = &operands;
```

is declared, then

```
ptr_operands -> push('A');
```

invokes the member function `push`, which has the effect of incrementing `operands.top` and setting `operands.s[top]` to `'A'`. One last observation: The member function `top_of` had its name changed from the previous implementation because of a naming conflict.

Member functions that are defined within the `struct` are implicitly inline. As a rule, only short, heavily used member functions should be defined within the `struct`, as is the case for the example just given. To define a member function outside the `struct`, the scope resolution operator is used. Let us illustrate this by changing the definition of `push` to its corresponding function prototype within the `struct stack`. We write it out fully using the scope resolution operator. In this case the function is not implicitly inline.

```
struct stack {
   //data representation

   char s[max_len];
   int  top;
   enum {EMPTY = -1, FULL = max_len - 1};

   //operations represented as member functions

   void reset() { top = EMPTY; } //implicitly inline
   void push(char c);            //function prototype
   . . .
};

   void stack::push(char c)      //definition, not inline
   {
      top++;
      s[top] = c;
   }
```

The scope resolution operator allows member functions from the different `struct` types to have the same names. In this case, which member function is invoked will depend on the type of object it acts upon. Member functions within the same `struct` can be overloaded. Consider adding to the data type `stack` a pop operation that has an integer parameter that is the number of times the stack should be popped. It could be added as the following function prototype within the `struct`:

```
char pop(int n);                    //within stack

char stack::pop(int n)
{
    while(n-- > 1)
        top--;
    return (s[top--]);
}
```

The definition that is invoked depends on the actual arguments to pop.

```
data.pop();                         //invokes standard pop
data.pop(5);                        //invokes iterated pop
```

3.5 Visibility private and public

The concept of struct is augmented in C++ to allow functions to have public and private members. Inside a struct, the use of the keyword private followed by a colon restricts the scope of the members that follow this construct. The private members can be used by only a few categories of functions, whose privileges include access to these members. These functions include the member functions of the struct. Other categories of functions having access will be discussed later.

We modify our example of stack to hide its data representation.

```
struct stack {
private:
    char s[max_len];
    int  top;
    enum {EMPTY = -1, FULL = max_len - 1};
public:
    void    reset() { top = EMPTY; }
    void    push(char c) { top++; s[top] = c; }
    char    pop() { return (s[top--]); }
    char    top_of() { return (s[top]); }
    boolean empty() { return (boolean)(top == EMPTY); }
    boolean full() { return (boolean)(top == FULL); }
};
```

We now rewrite `main` from Section 3.3 to test the same operations.

```
main()
{
    stack   s;
    char    str[40] = {"My name is Don Knuth!"};
    int     i = 0;

    cout << str << "\n";
    s.reset();                  //s.top = EMPTY; would be illegal
    while (str[i])
        if (!s.full())
            s.push(str[i++]);
    while (!s.empty())          //print the reverse
        cout << s.pop();
    cout << "\n";
}
```

The output from this version of the test program is

```
My name is Don Knuth!
!htunK noD si eman yM
```

As the comment in `main` states, access to the hidden variable `top` is controlled. It can be changed by the member function `reset` but cannot be accessed directly. Also notice how the variable s is passed to each member function using the structure member operator form.

The `struct stack` has a private part that contains its data description and has a public part that contains member functions to implement stack operations. It is useful to think of the private part as restricted to the implementor's use, and the public part to be an interface specification that clients may use. At a later time, the implementor could change the private part without affecting the correctness of a client's use of the stack type.

Hiding data is an important component of OOP. It allows for more easily debugged and maintained code because errors and modifications are localized. Client programs need only be aware of the type's interface specification.

3.6 Classes

Classes in C++ are introduced by the keyword `class`. They are a form of `struct` whose default privacy specification is `private`. Thus `struct` and `class` can be used interchangeably with the appropriate privacy specification.

Many scientific computations require complex numbers. Let us write an ADT for complex numbers.

```
struct complex {
private:
    double real, imag;
public:
    void   assign(double r, double i);
    void   print() { cout << real << " + " << imag; }
};

void complex::assign(double r, double i = 0.0)
{
    real = r;
    imag = i;
}
```

Here is its equivalent `class` representation:

```
class complex {
    double real, imag;
public:
    void   assign(double r, double i);
    void   print() { cout << real << " + " << imag << "i "; }
};

void complex::assign(double r, double i = 0.0)
{
    real = r;
    imag = i;
}
```

Notice that the only difference is in the use of the keywords `public` and `private`. Also possible would have been

```
class complex {
private:          //one style is to make this explicit
   double real, imag;
public:
   void    assign(double r, double i);
   void    print() { cout << real << " + " << imag << "i "; }
};
```

It will be our style to prefer `class` to `struct` unless all members are to be treated as `public`.

3.7 `static` **Member**

Data members can be declared with the storage class modifier `static`. A data member that is declared `static` is shared by all variables of that class and is stored uniquely in one place. Because of this it can be accessed in the form

> *class name* : : *identifier*

provided it has `public` visibility. This is a further use of the scope resolution operator (see Section 2.5). A static member of a global class must be explicitly declared and defined in file scope. An example is

```
enum boolean {false, true};

class str {
   char          s[100];
public:
   static boolean  read_only;  //definition in file scope
   void            print();
   void            assign(const char*);
   . . .
};

boolean str::read_only = false; //definition and initialization
```

In our example, this could be used to decide whether an object of type `str` could be changed in value. So,

```
str s1, s2, s3, s4;
if (!str::read_only)
   s1.assign("Buzz Dolsberry");
```

is a means of conveniently maintaining a value common to the entire class. Classes with `static` members have some restrictions that will be explained in the next chapter.

3.8 Nested Classes

Classes can be nested. The rules for nesting classes are in transition. C++ Release 2.0 rules state that the inner class is not inside the scope of the outer class but rather has the same scope as the outer class. Since this can lead to confusion, nesting class declarations is normally poor style.

The following nested classes illustrate this:

```
char c;                 //external scope
class X {               //outer class declaration
    char c;
    class Y {           //inner class declaration
        char d;
        void foo(char e) { c = e; }
    };
    char goo(X* q) { return (q -> d); }   //illegal
};
```

In `class Y` the member function `foo`, when using `c`, means the external scope c. It is as if `class Y` were declared at the same level and inside the same block or file scope as `class X`. In `class X` the member function `goo`, when using `d`, is attempting to access a private member of `class Y`. New rules are being proposed that will make the inner class scoped within the outer class. The safest current policy is to avoid this construction.

3.9 An Example: Flushing

We wish to estimate the probability of being dealt a flush. A flush occurs when at least five cards are of the same suit. We simulate shuffling cards by using a random number generator to shuffle the deck. This is a form of *Monte Carlo* calculation. The program will be written using classes to represent the needed data types and functionality.

```
//A poker calculation on flushing

#include  <iostream.h>
#include  <stdlib.h>        //for random number generation
#include  <time.h>          //for random number seed

enum suit {clubs, diamonds, hearts, spades};

class pips {
   int  p;
public:
   void assign(int n) { p = n % 13 + 1; }
   int  getpip() { return (p); }
   void print();
};

class card {
   int  cd;                          //a cd is from 0 to 51
public:
   suit s;
   pips p;
   void assign(int n) { cd = n; (suit)(s = n/13); p.assign(n); }
   void pr_card();
};

class deck {
   card d[52];
public:
   void init_deck();
   void shuffle();
   void deal(int, int, card*);
   void pr_deck();
};
```

We used an enumerated type suit to represent card suits. The enumerated constants are mapped into the integers 0, 1, 2, and 3. So clubs is the
integer value 0, and spades is the integer value 3. Each level of declaration
hides the complexity of the previous level. Notice also that we can plan to
code the functions later. For example, we will not use the print routines in
this example; they can be added as needed.

A most interesting function is the implicitly inline function

```
void assign(int n) { cd = n; (suit)(s = n/13); p.assign(n); }
```

which uses the function void pips::assign(int n);. We could have
used the notation p.pips::assign(n) to show clearly that this function is

from the class `pips`, but this is unnecessary. The function maps an integer whose value is between 0 and 51 into a unique pair of `suit` and `pips` values. The value 0 becomes the ace of clubs, and the value 51 becomes the king of spades.

The other member functions are not inline and are defined at a later point with the use of the scope resolution operator.

```
void   deck::init_deck()
{
    for (int i = 0; i < 52; ++i)
        d[i].assign(i);
}

void   deck::shuffle()
{
    for (int i = 0; i < 52; ++i) {
        int k = rand() % 52;
        card t = d[i]; d[i] = d[k]; d[k] = t; //swap two cards
    }
}

void deck::deal(int n, int pos, card* hand)
{
    for (int i = pos; i < pos + n; ++i)
        hand[i - pos] = d[i];
}
```

The init_deck function calls `card::assign` to map the integers into card values. The `shuffle` function uses the library-supplied pseudo-random number generator `rand` to exchange two cards for every deck position. Tests show that this gives a reasonable approximation to good shuffling. The `deal` function takes cards in sequence from the deck and arranges them into hands.

It now remains to use these functions to estimate the probability that a flush occurs when poker hands are dealt. The operator can choose to deal between five and nine cards per hand.

```
main()
{
    card one_hand[9];            //max hand is 9 cards
    deck dk;
    int  i, j, k, fcnt = 0, sval[4];
    int  ndeal, nc, nhand;
```

```
    do {
        cout << "\nEnter no. of cards in each hand (5-9): ";
        cin >> nc;
    } while (nc < 5 || nc > 9);
    nhand = 52 / nc;

    cout << "\nEnter no. of hands to deal: ";
    cin >> ndeal;

    randomize():
    dk.init_deck();
    for (k = 0; k < ndeal; k += nhand) {
        if ((nhand + k) > ndeal)
            nhand = ndeal - k;
        dk.shuffle();
        for (i = 0; i < nc * nhand; i += nc) {
            for (j = 0; j < 4; ++j)          //init suit counts to 0
                sval[j] = 0;
            dk.deal(nc, i, one_hand);        //deal next hand
            for (j = 0; j < nc; ++j)
                sval[one_hand[j].s] ++ ;     //increment suit count
            for (j = 0; j < 4; ++j)
                if (sval[j] >= 5)            //5 or more is flush
                    fcnt++;
        }
    }
    cout << "\n\nIn " << ndeal << " ";
    cout << nc << "-card hands there were ";
    cout << fcnt << " flushes\n   ";
}
```

DISSECTION OF THE *flush* PROGRAM

```
card one_hand[9];                    //max hand is 9 cards
deck dk;
int  i, j, k, fcnt = 0, sval[4];
int  ndeal, nc, nhand;
```

■ These are variables allocated upon block entry when main is executed. The variable one_hand is an array of nine elements, the

maximum hand size allowed. It will be used to store dealt-out hands from the deck. The variable dk represents our deck and is automatically allocated. All its data members are created, though some are hidden. The number of cards dealt to each hand is stored as the variable nc, and the number of hands to be dealt is kept in the variable ndeal. The variable fcnt will count the number of flushes. The array sval is used to store the number of cards found in the hand of a particular suit value.

```
do {
    cout << "\nEnter no. of cards in each hand (5-9): ";
    cin  >> nc;
} while (nc < 5 || nc > 9);
nhand = 52 / nc;

cout << "\nEnter no. of hands to deal: ";
cin  >> ndeal;
```

■ We prompt for the number of cards to deal to each hand. The operator must respond with a number between 5 and 9 in order to proceed. The number of hands that can be dealt with the deck is computed and put into the variable nhand. We prompt for the number of deals.

```
randomize();
dk.init_deck();
for (k = 0; k < ndeal; k += nhand) {
    if ((nhand + k) > ndeal)
        nhand = ndeal - k;
    dk.shuffle();
```

■ The rand function is initialized by randomize, which uses the system clock information made available in *time.h*. The deck variable dk is initialized, and each time through the main loop the deck is reshuffled. The variable dk is implicitly an argument to the called member functions init_deck and shuffle. The test to check whether the value of ndeal has been exceeded ensures that the total number of hands dealt will not exceed the request if the total number of hands is not an even multiple of the number of hands per shuffle.

```
for (i = 0; i < nc * nhand; i += nc) {
   for (j = 0; j < 4; ++j)                 //init suit counts to 0
      sval[j] = 0;
   dk.deal(nc, i, one_hand);               //deal next hand
   for (j = 0; j < nc; ++j)
      sval[one_hand[j].s] ++;              //increment suit count
   for (j = 0; j < 4; ++j)
      if (sval[j] >= 5)                    //5 or more is flush
         fcnt++;
}
```

■ The array `sval` stores the number of cards of each suit and is initialized to zero for each hand. The function `deck::deal` deals a card hand into the array `one_hand`. The expression `one_hand[j].s` is the suit value of a particular card—for example, 0 if the card were a club. This then is the index of the array `sval` that counts suits. The variable `fcnt` counts the number of flushes dealt over all these trials. Since the number of trials equals `ndeal`, the expectation of a flush is `fcnt/ndeal` .

3.10 Turbo C++ Considerations

In generating random number sequences, we have used the function `randomize` found in the Turbo C++ version of *stdlib.h*. This is not required by the ANSI standard. It is used to call `srand` as a means of seeding the random number sequence with a call to `time` found in *time.h*. It is defined as the macro

```
#define randomize()     srand((unsigned)time(NULL))
```

This uses the elapsed time in seconds since January 1, 1970, to initialize the seed for `rand`.

Enumerations

In this and other chapters, we have frequently used casts to convert an integer valued expression to a specific enumeration type.

```
enum boolean {false, true};

boolean empty(const stack* stk)
{
    return (boolean)(stk -> top == EMPTY);
}
```

The equality expression evaluates as an integer. This is a wider type than an enumeration. All enumerations are distinct types. It has been past practice to assign integer values to enumeration variables. This is technically illegal without a cast. It currently results in a compile time warning message and at a later point may be forbidden. Implicit conversion from an enumeration type to an integer value is a widening and is allowed in expressions.

The above declaration of `boolean` is an external file scope declaration. It allows `boolean` variable declarations within its scope, as well as the use of the enumerators `false` and `true`. If the enumeration were declared inside a class, as in

```
class foo_bool {
public:
    enum boolean {false, true} flag;
};

main()
{
    boolean  b = foo_bool::true;   //legal under 2.0 rules
    foo_bool c;
    c.flag = false;  //illegal need foo_bool::false
    . . .
}
```

the enumerators have class scope, but `boolean` is a global type as currently defined by Release 2.0. This is expected to change when new rules for nesting are implemented. For the moment, it is best to avoid these nested declarations.

Use of const Arguments

C++ and ANSI C introduce the `const` modifier. One of its chief uses occurs in function declarations. Ordinary C and C++ arguments are call-by-value, meaning they are not modifiable. Upon function invocation, actual arguments are evaluated and copied onto the local stack to be manipulated internally by the function. Aggregate data, such as arrays and structures, can be expensive to copy and can be more efficiently passed by reference or indirectly as a pointer. When it is desirable to indicate that such data are non-modifiable, the `const` modifier is used. It enhances code reliability and might prove useful to code optimization by the compiler.

Summary

1. The original name given by Stroustrup to his language was "C with classes." A `class` is an extension of the idea of `struct` in traditional C. It is a way of implementing a data type and associated functions and operators. It also is the mechanism in C++ for implementing ADTs, such as complex numbers and stacks.

2. The structure type allows the programmer to aggregate components into a single named variable. A structure has components, called *members*, that are individually named. Critical to processing structures is the accessing of their members. This is done with either the member operator " . " or the structure pointer operator `->`. These operators, along with `()` and `[]`, have the highest precedence.

3. The concept of `struct` is augmented in C++ to allow functions to be members. The function declaration is included in the structure declaration and is invoked by using access methods for structure members. The idea is that the functionality required by the `struct` data type should be directly included in the `struct` declaration.

4. Member functions that are defined within the `struct` are implicitly inline. As a rule, only short, heavily used member functions should be defined within the `struct`. To define a member function outside the `struct`, the scope resolution operator is used.

5. The scope resolution operator allows member functions from the different `struct` types to have the same names. In this case, which member function is invoked will depend on the type of object it acts upon. Member functions within the same `struct` can be overloaded.

6. The concept of `struct` is augmented in C++ to allow functions to have `public` and `private` members. This provides *data hiding*. Inside a `struct`, the use of the keyword `private` followed by a colon restricts the scope of the members that follow this construct. The `private` mem-

bers can be used by only a few categories of functions, whose privileges include access to these members. These functions include the member functions of the `struct`.

7. Classes in C++ are introduced by the keyword `class`. They are a form of `struct` whose default privacy specification is `private`. Thus `struct` and `class` can be used interchangeably with the appropriate privacy specification.

8. Data members can be declared with the storage class modifier `static`. A data member that is declared `static` is shared by all variables of that class and is stored uniquely in one place. Because of this it can be accessed in the form

    > *class name* `: :` *identifier*

9. Classes can be nested. The inner class is not inside the scope of the outer class but rather has the same scope as the outer class. This is not a recommended practice.

Exercises

1. Design a traditional C structure to store a dairy product name, portion weight, calories, protein, fat, and carbohydrates. Twenty-five grams of American cheese has 375 calories, 5 grams of protein, 8 grams of fat, and 0 grams of carbohydrates. Show how to assign these values to the member variables of your structure. Write a function that, given a variable of type `struct dairy` and a given weight in grams (portion size), returns the number of calories for that weight.

2. Use the `struct card` defined in Section 3.1 and write a hand-sorting routine. In card games, most players keep their cards sorted by pip value. The routine will place aces first, kings next, and so forth, down to twos. A hand will be five cards.

3. The following declarations do not compile correctly. Explain what is wrong.

    ```
    struct brother {
        char          name[20];
        int           age;
        struct sister sib;
    } a;
    ```

```
struct sister {
    char           name[20];
    int            age;
    struct brother sib;
} a;
```

4. In this exercise, use the `struct stack` defined in Section 3.3. Write the function

   ```
   void reverse(char s1[], char s2[]);
   ```

   The strings `s1` and `s2` must be the same size. String `s2` should become a reversed copy of string `s1`. Internal to `reverse`, use a `stack` to perform the reversal.

5. Rewrite the functions `push` and `pop` in Section 3.3 to test that `push` is not acting on a full stack and `pop` is not acting on an empty stack. If either condition is detected, print an error message using `cerr`, and use `exit(1)` (in *stdlib.h*) to abort the program.

6. Write `reverse` (see Exercise 4) as a member function for type `stack` in Section 3.4. Test it by printing normally and reversed the string

   ```
   Gottfried Leibniz wrote Toward a Universal Characteristic
   ```

7. For the `stack` type in Section 3.4, write as member functions

   ```
   //push n chars from s1[1] onto the stack
   void pushm(int n, const char s1[]);

   //pop n chars from stack into char string
   void popm(int n, char s1[]);
   ```

   Hint: Be sure to put a terminator character into the string before outputting it.

8. What is the difference in meaning between the structure

   ```
   struct a {
       int i, j, k;
   };
   ```

   and the class

   ```
   class a {
       int i, j, k;
   };
   ```

Explain why the class declaration is not useful. How can you use the keyword `public` to change the class declaration into a declaration equivalent to `struct a`?

9. We wish to define the class `deque` to implement a double-ended queue. A double-ended queue allows push and pop at both ends.

```
class deque {
    char s[max_len];
    int  bottom, top;
public:
    void reset() { top = bottom = max_len / 2; top--; }
    ...
};
```

Declare and implement `push_t`, `pop_t`, `push_b`, `pop_b`, `out_stack`, `top_of`, `bottom_of`, `empty`, and `full`. The function `push_t` stands for *push on top*. The function `push_b` stands for *push on bottom*. The `out_stack` function should output the stack from its bottom to its top. The `pop_t` and `pop_b` functions correspond to *pop from top* and *pop from bottom*. An empty stack is denoted by having the top fall below the bottom. Test each function.

10. Extend the data type `deque` by adding a member function `relocate`. If the `deque` is full, then `relocate` is called, and the contents of the deque are moved to balance empty storage around the center `max_len / 2` of array s. Its function declaration header is

```
//returns true if it succeeds, false if it fails
boolean deque::relocate()
```

11. Write a swap function that swaps the contents of two strings. If you pushed a string of characters onto a stack and popped them into a second string, they would come out reversed. In a swap of two strings, we want the original ordering. Use a `deque` to swap two strings. The strings will be stored in two character arrays of the same length, but the strings themselves may be of differing lengths. The function prototype is

```
void swap(char s1[], char s2[]);
```

12. Write the following member functions:

```
void pips::print();
void card::pr_card();
void deck::pr_deck();
```

and add them to the *flush* program found in Section 3.9. Let `pr_deck` use `pr_card` and `pr_card` use `print`. Print the deck after it is initialized.

13. Write a function `pr_hand` that prints out card hands. Add it to the *flush* program, and use it to print out each flush.

14. In Section 3.9, `main` detects flushes. Write a function

    ```
    boolean isflush(const card hand[], int nc);
    ```

    that returns `true` if a `hand` is a flush.

15. Write a function

    ```
    boolean isstraight(const card hand[], nc);
    ```

    that returns `true` if a `hand` is a straight. A straight is five cards that have sequential pips value. The lowest straight is ace, two, three, four, five, and the highest straight is ten, jack, queen, king, ace. Run experiments to estimate the probability that dealt-out cards will be a straight, and compare the results of five-card hands with results of seven-card hands.

    Hint: You may want to set up an array of 15 integers to correspond to counters for each pips value. Be sure that a pip value of 1 (corresponding to aces) is also counted as the high card corresponding to a pip value of 14.

16. Use the previous exercises to determine the probability that a poker hand will be a straight flush. This is a hand that is both a straight and flush. It is the hardest poker hand to get and has the highest value. Note that, in a hand of more than five cards, it is not sufficient to merely check for the presence of both a straight and a flush to determine that the hand is a straight flush.

17. Change the `suit` declaration from an enumerated type to a class as follows:

    ```
    enum {clubs, diamonds, hearts, spades};

    class suit {
       enum {clubs, diamonds, hearts, spades} s;
    public:
       void assign(int n) { s = n / 13; }
       int  getsuit() { return (s); }
       void print();
    };
    ```

We use an anonymous `enum` to define the four integer constants used for suit values. We add the member function `getsuit` to access the hidden integer value of a `suit` variable. Now recode all references to `suit` throughout the program.

Chapter 4

Constructors
and Destructors

A constructor is a member function whose name is the same as the class name. It *constructs* values of the class type. This process involves initializing of data members and, frequently, allocating free store using `new`. A destructor is a member function whose name is the class name preceded by the character ~ (tilde). Its usual purpose is to *destroy* values of the class type, typically by using `delete`.

Constructors are the more complicated of these two specially named member functions. They may be overloaded and can take arguments, neither

91

of which is possible for destructors. Constructors are invoked when their associated type is used in a declaration. They are also invoked when call-by-value is used to pass a value to a function. Constructors and destructors do not have return types and cannot use `return` statements. Destructors are implicitly invoked when an object of its class must be destroyed, typically upon block exit or function exit.

4.1 Classes with Constructors

The simplest use of a constructor is for initialization. We shall develop some examples in this and later sections that use constructors to initialize the values of the data members of the class.

Our first example is an implementation of a data type `mod_int` to store numbers that are computed with a modulus.

```
// Modulo numbers and constructor initialization

#include <iostream.h>

const int modulus = 60;
class mod_int {
    int   v;
public:
    mod_int(int i) { v = i % modulus; }
    void assign(int i) { v = i % modulus; }
    void print() { cout << v << "\t"; }
};
```

The integer v will be restricted in value to 0, 1, 2, ... modulus − 1. It is the programmer's responsibility to enforce this restriction by having all member functions guarantee this behavior. The member function `mod_int` is a constructor. It does not have a return type. Some examples of declarations using this type are:

```
mod_int   a(0);    // a.v = 0;
mod_int   b(61);   // b.v = 1;
```

but not

```
mod_int   a;        // no parameter list
```

Using this type, we can write code to convert seconds into minutes and seconds as follows.

```
main()
{
    int      seconds = 400;
    mod_int z(seconds);

    cout << seconds << " seconds equals "
        << seconds / 60 << " minutes ";
    z.print();
    cout << " seconds\n";
}
```

It is often convenient to overload the constructor with several function declarations. In our example, it could be desirable to have the default value of v be 0. By adding the constructor

```
mod_int() { v = 0; }
```

as a member function of mod_int, it is possible to have the following declarations:

```
mod_int s1, s2;  // both initialize the private member v to 0
mod_int d[5];    // arrays are properly initialized
```

In both of these declarations, the empty parameter list constructor is invoked. This is called the *default* constructor.

A constructor can also be used to allocate space from free store. We shall modify the stack type from Chapter 3 to have its maximum length be initialized by a constructor.

```
//stack implementation with constructor
class stack {
   enum  {EMPTY = -1};
   char* s;           //changed from s[max_len]
   int    max_len;
   int    top;
public:
   //the public interface for the ADT stack
   stack(int size) { s = new char[size];
                     max_len = size; top = EMPTY; }
   void reset() { top = EMPTY; }
   void push(char c) { top++; s[top] = c; }
   char pop() { return (s[top--]); }
   char top_of() { return (s[top]); }
   boolean empty() { return (boolean)(top == EMPTY;) }
   boolean full() { return (boolean)(top == max_len - 1); }
};
```

An example of a `stack` declaration invoking this constructor is:

```
stack data(1000);    // allocate 1000 element char stack
```

Two alternate constructors would be an empty parameter constructor that would allocate a specific length stack and a two-parameter constructor whose second parameter is a string used to initialize the stack. They could be written as follows:

```
stack::stack()
{
   s = new char[100];
   max_len = 100;
   top = EMPTY;
}

stack::stack(int size, const char str[])
{
   s = new char[size];
   max_len = size;
   for ( int i = 0; i < max_len && str[i] != 0; ++i)
      s[i] = str[i];
   top = --i;
}
```

The corresponding function prototypes would be included as members of the class `stack`.

4.2 Classes with Destructors

Destructors are member functions whose name is the same as the class name preceded by a tilde. They cannot be explicitly called and usually are associated with classes where data members are dynamically allocated from free store.

Let us augment our stack example with a destructor.

```
//stack implementation with constructors and destructor
class stack {
    enum  {EMPTY = -1};
    char* s;
    int   max_len;
    int   top;
public:
    stack(int size) { s = new char[size];
                      max_len = size; top = EMPTY; }
    stack();
    stack(int size, const char str[]);
    ~stack() { delete s; }    //destructor
    ...
};
```

The external interface of this class remains the same. In other words, all the public member functions perform in exactly the same manner as before. The difference is that the destructor will be implicitly invoked upon block and function exit to clean up storage that is no longer accessible. This is good programming practice and allows programs to execute with less available memory.

4.3 An Example: Dynamically Allocated Strings

A string type is lacking in traditional C. Strings in C are represented as pointer to char and are manipulated accordingly. In this representation, the end-of-string is denoted by \0. This convention has an important drawback, in that many basic string manipulations are proportional to string length. When the string length is known, the efficiency of operations on strings can be significantly improved.

We shall develop a useful string ADT in this section that stores its length privately. We want our type to be dynamically allocated and able to represent arbitrary length strings. A variety of constructors will be coded to initialize and allocate strings, and a set of operations on strings will be coded as member functions. The implementation will use the `string.h` library functions to manipulate the underlying pointer representation of strings.

```
//An implementation of dynamically allocated strings.
#include <string.h>
#include <iostream.h>

class string {
   char* s;
   int   len;
public:
   string() { s = new char[81]; len = 80; }
   string(int n) { s = new char[n + 1]; len = n; }
   string(const char* p) { len = strlen(p);
                           s = new char[len + 1];
                           strcpy(s, p); }
   string(const string& str);
   ~string() { delete s; }
   void assign(const char* str) { strcpy(s, str);
                                  len = strlen(str); }
   void print() { cout << s << "\n"; }
   void concat(const string& a, const string& b);
};

string::string(const string& str)
{
   len = str.len;
   s = new char[len + 1];
   strcpy(s, str.s);
}

void string::concat(const string& a, const string& b)
{
   len = a.len + b.len;
   delete s;
   s = new char[len + 1];
   strcpy(s, a.s);
   strcat(s, b.s);
}
```

This type allows you to declare strings, assign a character array to a string, print a string, and concatenate two strings. The hidden representation is pointer to `char` and has a variable `len` in which to store the current string length. The constructors all allocate dynamically from free store.

DISSECTION OF THE *string* CLASS

```
string() { s = new char[81]; len = 80; }
string(int n) { s = new char[n + 1]; len = n; }
string(const char* p) { len = strlen(p);
                        s = new char[len + 1];
                        strcpy(s, p); }
string(const string& str);
```

■ There are four overloaded constructors. The first is the empty parameter default. This is used to declare an array of strings. The second has an `int` parameter that is used to initialize the string length variable `len` and to retrieve that much store using `new`. The third constructor has a pointer to `char` argument that can be used to transform the traditional C representation of strings to our `class` type. It uses two library functions: `strlen` and `strcpy`. We allocate one additional character to store the end-of-string character \0, although this character is not counted by `strlen`. The fourth constructor will be explained below.

```
string() { delete s; }
```

■ The destructor automatically returns memory allocated to strings back to free store for reuse. The operator `delete` knows the amount of memory associated with the pointer s as base address.

```
void assign(const char* str) { strcpy(s, str);
                               len = strlen(str); }
void print() { cout << s << "\n"; }
```

■ These two inline member functions provide an assignment and print operation, respectively. The assignment takes the traditional C representation pointer to `char` and uses `strcpy` to copy this to the private member variable s.

```
string::string(const string& str)
{
    len = str.len;
    s = new char[len + 1];
    strcpy(s, str.s);
}
```

■ This form of constructor is used to perform copying of one string value into another when:

1. A string is initialized by another string.

2. A string is passed as an argument in a function.

3. A string is returned as the value of a function.

In Turbo C++, if this constructor is not present, then these operations are member by member assignment of value.

```
void string::concat(const string& a, const string& b)
{
    len = a.len + b.len;
    delete s;
    s = new char[len + 1];
    strcpy(s, a.s);
    strcat(s, b.s);
}
```

■ This is a form of string concatenation. The two string arguments are not modified. The implicit argument, whose hidden member variables are s and len, is modified to represent the string a followed by the string b. Note that in this member function the use of len, a.len, and b.len is possible. Member functions have access not only to the private members of the implicit argument but also to the private representation of any of the arguments.

The following code tests this type by concatenating several strings:

```
main()
{
    char*   str = "The wheel that squeaks the loudest\n";
    string  a(str), b, author("Josh Billings\n"), both, quote;
```

```
    b.assign("Is the one that gets the grease\n");
    both.concat(a, b);
    quote.concat(both, author);
    quote.print();
}
```

The printout from this program is:

```
The wheel that squeaks the loudest
Is the one that gets the grease
Josh Billings
```

We deliberately used a variety of declarations to show how different constructors would be called. The string variables b, both, and quote all use the empty argument list constructor. The declaration for author uses the constructor whose argument type is char*, which is the type of a literal C string. The concatenation takes place in two steps. First, strings a and b are concatenated into both. Next, strings both and author are concatenated into quote. It is important to understand that both is an argument to con-cat and is used internally wherever the unqualified member names are written.

4.4 A Class vect

The one-dimensional array in C is a very useful efficient aggregate type. However, the traditional C array is error prone. A common mistake is to access elements that are *out of bounds*. C++ allows us to control this problem by defining an analogous array type in which bounds can be tested.

```
//Implementation of a safe array type vect
#include <iostream.h>
#include <stdlib.h>      //for exit

class vect {
    int* p;
    int  size;
public:
    int  ub;            //upper bound = size - 1
    vect() { size = 10; p = new int[size]; ub = size - 1; }
    vect(int n);
    ~vect() { delete p; }
    int& element(int i);
};
```

```
vect::vect(int n)
{
   if (n <= 0) {
      cerr << "illegal vect size " << n << "\n";
      exit(1);
   }
   size = n;
   p = new int[size];
   ub = size - 1;
}


int& vect::element(int i)
{
   if (i < 0 || i > ub) {
      cerr << "illegal vect index " << i << "\n";
      exit(1);
   }
   return (p[i]);
}
```

The constructor `vect::vect(int n)` allows the user to build dynamically allocated arrays. Such arrays are much more flexible than those in traditional C, where array sizes must be constant expressions. The constructor also initializes the variable `ub`, whose value is the array upper bound. Access to individual elements is through the safe indexing member function

```
int& vect::element(int i)
```

An index that is outside the expected array range 0 through `ub` will cause an error message and error exit. This safe indexing member function returns a reference to `int` that is the address of `p[i]` and that can be used as the left operand of an assignment or *lvalue*. The technique is much used in C++ and will be an efficient mechanism for operating on complicated types.

As an example, the declarations

```
vect a(10), b(5);
```

construct an array of ten integers and an array of five integers, respectively. Individual elements can be accessed by the member function `element`, which checks whether the index is out of range. The statements

```
a.element(1) = 5;
b.element(1) = a.element(1) + 7;
cout << a.element(1) - 2;
```

are all legal. In effect we have a safe dynamic array type.

Classes with default constructors use them to initialize a derived array type. For example,

```
vect a[5];
```

is a declaration that uses the empty argument constructor to create an array a of five objects, each of which is a size 10 vect. The ith element's address in the jth array would be given by a[j].element(i).

4.5 Members That Are Class Types

In this section we shall use the type vect as part of a new class. We wish to store multiple values for each index. For example, we may want to store the age, weight, and height of a group of individuals. We could group three arrays together inside a new class.

```
#include "vect.h"

class multi_v {
public:
    vect a, b, c;
    multi_v(int i) : a(i), b(i), c(i) { }
};
```

The class has three vect members and a constructor, which has an empty body but a list of constructor calls separated by commas. These constructors are executed with the integer argument i creating the three class objects a, b, and c. In early versions of the C++ language, the order of constructor invocation was unspecified. In newer versions, the order is as written in the comma-separated list followed by any default initializations.

Let us test this class by writing code to store and print a set of values for age in years, weight in pounds, and height in inches.

```
main()
{
    multi_v a_w_h(5);    //age weight and height

    for (int i = 0; i <= a_w_h.a.ub; ++i) {
        a_w_h.a.element(i) = 21 + i;
        a_w_h.b.element(i) = 135 + i;
        a_w_h.c.element(i) = 62 + i;
    }
    for (i = 0; i <= a_w_h.a.ub; ++i) {
        cout << a_w_h.a.element(i) << " years ";
        cout << a_w_h.b.element(i) << " pounds ";
        cout << a_w_h.c.element(i) << " inches\n";
    }
}
```

The declaration of a_w_h creates three vect members each of five elements. When the program is executed, the individual destructors for each vect member will be called upon block exit from main. The ordering of destructor calls in newer C++ systems is to be the reverse of the call on constructors. When executed, the above program will print:

```
21 years 135 pounds 62 inches
22 years 136 pounds 63 inches
23 years 137 pounds 64 inches
24 years 138 pounds 65 inches
25 years 139 pounds 66 inches
```

4.6 An Example: A Singly Linked List

In this section, we develop a singly linked list data type. This is the prototype of many useful dynamic data structures called *self-referential* structures. These data types have pointer members that refer to objects of their own type. A linked list is like a clothes line on which the data elements hang sequentially. The head of the line is the only immediate access point, and items can readily be added to or deleted from it. The following class declaration implements such a type.

```
//A singly linked list

#include <iostream.h>

struct listelem {
    char        data;
    listelem*   next;
};
```

```
class list {
    listelem*   h;              //head of list
public:
    list() { h = 0; }           //0 is the NULL pointer value
    ~list() { release(); }
    void add(char c);           //adds to front of list
    void del() { listelem* temp = h;
                 h = h -> next;
                 delete temp; }
    listelem* first() { return (h); }
    void pr_list();
    void release();
};
```

The link member `next` is self-referential. The variable `data` in this example is a simple variable, but it could be replaced by a complicated type capable of storing a range of information. The constructor initializes the head of list pointer `h` to the value 0, which is called the *null pointer constant.* It can be assigned to any pointer type. In linked lists it typically denotes the empty list or end-of-list value. The member function `add` is used to build the list structure.

```
void list::add(char c)
{
    listelem* temp = new listelem;   //create new element

    temp -> next = h;                //link to list
    temp -> data = c;
    h = temp;                        //update head of list
}
```

A list element is allocated from free store, and its data member is initialized from the single argument `c`. Its link member `next` points at the old head of list. The head pointer `h` is then updated to point at this element as the new first element of the list.

The inline member function `del` has the inverse role. It returns the first element of the list to free store. It does this by using the `delete` operator on the head of list pointer `h`. The new head of list is the value of the `next` member.

Much of list processing is repetitively chaining down the list until the null pointer value is found. The following two functions use this technique.

```
void list::pr_list()
{
    listelem*  temp = h;

    while (temp != 0) {              //detect end of list
        cout << temp -> data << " -> ";
        temp = temp -> next;
    }
    cout << "\n###\n";
}

void list::release()  //elements are returned to free store
{
    while (h != 0)
        del();
}
```

DISSECTION OF THE *pr_list* AND *release* FUNCTIONS

```
void list::pr_list()
{
    listelem*  temp = h;
```

■ An auxiliary pointer `temp` will be used to chain down the list. It is initialized to the address of the list head `h`. The pointer `h` cannot be used because its value would be lost, in effect destroying access to the list.

```
while (temp != 0) {                      //detect end of list
    cout << temp -> data << " -> ";
    temp = temp -> next;
}
```

■ The value 0 represents the end-of-list value. It is guaranteed to be such because the constructor `list::list` initialized it and the `list::add` function maintains it as the end-of-list pointer value. Notice that the internals of this loop could be changed to process the entire list in some other manner.

```
void list::release()  //each element is returned to free store
```

- The `release` function is used to return all list elements to free store. It marches down the list doing so.

```
while (h != 0)
    del();
```

- Each element of the list must be returned to free store in sequence. This is done for a single element by the member function `del`, which manipulates the hidden pointer `h`. Since we are destroying the list, it is unnecessary to preserve the original value of pointer `h`. This function's chief use is as the body of the destructor `list::~list`. We could not use a destructor written

```
list::~list()
{
    delete h;
}
```

because it only deletes the first element in the list.

We demonstrate the use of this type in the following code:

```
main()
{
    list*  p;
    {
        list       w;

        w.add('A');
        w.add('B');
        w.pr_list();
        w.del();
        w.pr_list();
        p = &w;
        p -> pr_list();
    }
    p -> pr_list();
}
```

Notice that there is an inner block in `main`. That block is included to test that the destructor is invoked upon block exit, returning storage associated with `w` to free store. The output of this program is:

```
B -> A ->
###
A ->
###
A ->
###

###
```

The first `pr_list` call prints the two-element list storing B and A. After a `del` operation is performed, the list contains one element storing A. The outer block pointer to `list` p is assigned the address of the `list` variable w. When the list is accessed through p in the inner block, it prints A. After block exit, the same print command prints the empty list. This output shows that the destructor works at block exit on the variable w.

4.7 Two-Dimensional Arrays

Traditional C does not have authentic higher dimensional arrays. Instead, the programmer must be careful to map such an abstract data structure into a pointer to pointer to ... base type. In C++, the programmer can implement flexible safe dynamic higher dimensional arrays. We shall demonstrate this by implementing a two-dimensional array type `matrix`. The observant reader will notice the strong parallels with the class `vect`.

```
//A two-dimensional safe array type matrix
#include <iostream.h>
#include <stdlib.h>      //for exit

class matrix {
    int**   p;
    int     s1, s2;
public:
    int     ub1, ub2;
    matrix(int d1, int d2);
    ~matrix();
    int& element(int i, int j);
};
```

The type `matrix` has a size for each dimension and a corresponding public upper bound. The hidden representation uses the pointer to pointer to `int` type. This will store the base address of an array of pointers to `int` that in turn store a base address for each row of the `matrix` type.

```
matrix::matrix(int d1, int d2)
{
    if (d1 < 0 || d2 < 0) {
        cerr << "illegal matrix size "
            << d1 << " by " << d2 << "\n";
        exit(1);
    }
    s1 = d1;
    s2 = d2;
    p = new int*[s1];
    for (int i = 0; i < s1; ++i)
        p[i] = new int[s2];
    ub1 = s1 - 1;
    ub2 = s2 - 1;
}

matrix::~matrix()
{
    for (int i = 0; i <= ub1; ++i)
        delete p[i];
    delete p;
}
```

What is novel here are the ways the constructor and destructor work. The constructor allocates an array of pointer to `int`. The number of elements in this array is the value of `s1`. Next the constructor iteratively allocates an array of `int` pointed at by each element `p[i]`. Therefore there is space for `s1 * s2` integers allocated from free store, and additionally the space for `s1` pointers is allocated from free store. The destructor deallocates store in the reverse order. All of this generalizes to higher dimensions.

Obtaining the reference to (lvalue of) an element in this two-dimensional array requires two index arguments.

```
int& matrix::element(int i, int j)
{
    if (i < 0 || i > ub1 || j < 0 || j > ub2) {
        cerr << "illegal matrix index "
            << ub1 << ", " << ub2 << "\n";
        exit(1);
    }
    return (p[i][j]);
}
```

Both arguments are tested to see that they are in range. This is a generalization of the one index case.

4.8 The `this` **Pointer**

The keyword `this` denotes an implicitly declared self-referential pointer. It can be used in a nonstatic member function. A simple illustration of its use is as follows:

```
// Use of the this pointer

#include <iostream.h>

class c_pair {
   char     c1, c2;
public:
   c_pair(char b) { c1 = 1 + (c2 = b); }
   c_pair increment() { c1++; c2++; return (*this); }
   unsigned where_am_I() { return ((unsigned)this); }
   void print() { cout << c1 << c2 << "\t"; }
};

main()
{
   c_pair  a('A'), b('B'), c('D');
   a.print();
   cout << " is at " << a.where_am_I() << "\n";
   b.print();
   cout << " is at " << b.where_am_I() << "\n";
   c.increment().print();
   cout << " is at " << c.where_am_I() << "\n";
}
```

The member function `increment` uses the implicitly provided pointer `this` to return the newly incremented value of both `c1` and `c2`. The member function `where_am_I` returns the address of the given object. The `this` keyword provides for a built-in self-referential pointer. It's as if `c_pair` implicitly declared the private member `c_pair* const this`.

Early C++ systems allowed memory management for objects to be controlled by assignment to the `this` pointer. Such code is obsolete because the `this` pointer is non-modifiable.

4.9 Turbo C++ Considerations

Turbo C++ allows `static` and `const` member functions. Earlier C++ systems had not always implemented these constructs. Their implementation can be understood in terms of `this` pointer access.

`static` **and** `const` **Member Functions**

An ordinary member function invoked as

```
object.mem(i, j, k);
```

has an explicit argument list `i`, `j`, `k` and an implicit argument list that are the members of *object*. The implicit arguments can be thought of as a list of arguments accessible through the `this` pointer. In contrast, a `static` member function cannot access any of the members using the `this` pointer. A `const` member function cannot modify its implicit arguments. The following example illustrates these differences:

```
//Salary calculation using
//static and constant member functions.

#include <iostream.h>

class salary {
    int       b_sal;
    int       your_bonus;
    static int all_bonus;   //declaration
public:
    salary(int b)  : b_sal(b) { }
    void calc_bonus(double perc) { your_bonus = b_sal * perc; }
    static void reset_all(int p) { all_bonus = p; }
    int comp_tot() const
          { return (b_sal + your_bonus + all_bonus); }
};

int salary::all_bonus = 100; //declaration and definition

main()
{
    salary w1(1000), w2(2000);

    w1.calc_bonus(0.2);
    w2.calc_bonus(0.15);
    salary::reset_all(400);
    cout << " w1 " << w1.comp_tot() << "  w2 " << w2.comp_tot() << "\n";
}
```

DISSECTION OF THE *salary* PROGRAM

```
class salary {
   int        b_sal;
   int        your_bonus;
   static int all_bonus;    //declaration
```

- There are three private data members. The `static` member `all_bonus` requires a file scope declaration. It can exist independently of any specific variables of type `salary` being declared.

```
salary(int b) : b_sal(b) { }
```

- This constructor uses the initializer syntax following the colon. It has the effect of assigning the value of `b` to the member `b_sal`. Thus the code body can be empty.

```
static void reset_all(int p) { all_bonus = p; }
```

- The modifier `static` comes before the function return-type. The `static` member can also be referred to as:

```
        salary::all_bonus
```

```
int comp_tot() const
    { return (b_sal + your_bonus + all_bonus); }
```

- The `const` modifier comes between the end of the argument list and the front of the code body. It indicates that no data member will have its value changed. As such it makes the code more robust. In effect it means that the self-referential pointer is passed as `const salary* const this`.

```
salary::reset_all(400);
```

- A `static` member function can be invoked using the scope resolution operator. It could also have been invoked as:

```
        w1.reset_all(400);
```

but this is misleading, in that there is nothing special about using the class variable `w1`.

Breakpoints and Debugging

The IDE provides very convenient source level debugging. It allows the programmer to set *breakpoints* in the source code. The run window has an option to stop on breakpoints. This can be combined with either inspecting variables or setting watches on variables so as to display their values at critical points in the running program.

Breakpoints are set by selecting this command from the debug window. The breakpoints are highlighted in their own window, and they can be added using the *edit* command within this window. A simple breakpoint is set by writing out the line number of the file window it appears in.

Watches are set by selecting this command from the debug window. Most often these are variable names. When the variable is a `class` or `struct`, the watch on that variable will display all its data member variables. More complete information is found using the inspect command. The inspect command will display the variable's location and its machine dependent representation. When using the run menu, the *F8* key allows you to step through the code and inspect and watch variables from breakpoint to breakpoint.

Summary

1. A constructor is a member function whose name is the same as the class name. It *constructs* objects of the class type. This process may involve initializing data members and allocating free store using `new`.

2. A destructor is a member function whose name is the class name preceded by the character ~ (tilde). Its usual purpose is to *destroy* values of the class type, typically by using `delete`.

3. A class with constructors that has a constructor with an empty argument list is said to have a *default* constructor. A class with a default constructor uses it to initialize array declarations, where no initialized values are explicitly given.

4. An example of a class with both a constructor and destructor is:

```
class stack {
   enum { EMPTY = -1};
   char* s;
   int    max_len;
   int    top;
public:
   stack(int size) { s = new char[size];
                       max_len = size; top = EMPTY; }
   ~stack() { delete s; }
   ...
};
```

5. A constructor of the form

   ```
   type::type(type& x)
   ```

   is used to perform copying of one *type* value into another when:

   a. A *type* variable is initialized by a *type* value.

   b. A *type* value is passed as an argument in a function.

   c. A *type* value is returned from a function.

   In Turbo C++, if this constructor is not present, then these operations are member by member assignment of value. In older C++ systems, if this constructor is not present, then these operations are bitwise copy.

6. Classes with constructors having an empty argument list can have a derived array type. For example, in Section 4.4,

   ```
   vect a[5];
   ```

   is a declaration that uses the empty argument constructor to create an array a of five objects, each of which is a size 10 vect.

7. A class having members whose type requires a constructor may have these specified after the argument list for its own constructor. The constructor has a comma-separated list of constructor calls following a colon. The constructor is invoked by using the member name followed by an argument list in parentheses. In early versions of the C++ language, the order of constructor invocation was unspecified. In newer versions, the order is as written in the comma-separated list, followed by any default initializations.

8. A singly linked list is the prototype of many useful dynamic data structures called *self-referential* structures. A linked list is like a clothesline on which the data elements hang sequentially. The head of the line is the only immediate access point, and items can readily be added to or deleted from this point.

9. The value 0 is called the *null pointer constant.* It can be assigned to any pointer type. In linked lists, it typically denotes the empty list or end-of-list value.

10. The keyword `this` denotes an implicitly declared self-referential pointer. The `this` pointer can be used only inside a class member function to refer to non-statically declared members.

Exercises

1. Discuss why constructors are almost always `public` member functions. What goes wrong if they are `private`?

2. Write a member function for the class `mod_int`

   ```
   void add_to(int i);    //add i to v modulo 60.
   ```

   It should add the number of seconds in `i` to the current value of `v` while retaining the modulo 60 feature of `v`.

3. Run the following program and explain its behavior. Placing debugging information inside constructors and destructors is a very useful step in developing efficient and correct classes.

   ```
   //Constructors and destructors invoked

   #include <iostream.h>

   class A {
      int xx;
   public:
      A(int n) { xx = n;
                 cout << "A(int " << n << ") called\n"; }
      A(double y) { xx = y + 0.5;
                    cout << "A(fl " << y << ") called\n"; }
      ~A() { cout << "~A() called A::xx = " << xx << "\n"; }
   };
   ```

```
main()
{
    cout << "enter main\n";
    int x = 14;
    float y = 17.3;
    A z(11), zz(11.5), zzz(0);

    zzz = A(x);
    zzz = A(y);
    cout << "exit main\n";
}
```

4. Add an empty parameter list constructor for `class A`.

```
A() { xx = 0; cout << "A() called\n"; }
```

Now modify the previous program by declaring an array of type A

```
A d[5];      //declares an array of 5 elements of type A
```

Assign the values 0, 1, 2, 3, and 4 to the data member `xx` of each `d[i]`. Run the program and explain its behavior.

5. Use the `stack` type in Section 4.1 in this exercise, and include the empty argument constructor to allocate a stack of 100 elements. Write a program that swaps the contents of two stacks, using an array of stacks to accomplish the job. The two stacks will be the first two stacks in the array. One method would be to use four stacks: `st[0]`, `st[1]`, `st[2]`, and `st[3]`. Push the contents of `st[1]` into `st[2]`. Push the contents of `st[0]` into `st[3]`. Push the contents of `st[3]` into `st[1]`. Push the contents of `st[2]` into `st[0]`. Verify that the stacks have their contents in the same order by implementing a print function that outputs all elements in the stack. Can this be done with three stacks only?

6. Add a constructor to the type `stack` with the following prototype:

```
stack::stack(const char* c);     //initialize from string array
```

7. Use the `string` type in Section 4.3 in this exercise, and code the following member functions:

```
//strcmp is negative if s < s1,
//         is 0 if s == s1,
//         and is positive if s > s1
//         where s is the implicit string argument
int string::strcmp(const string& s1);
```

```
//strrev  reverses the implicit string argument
void string::strrev();

//print  is overloaded to print the first n characters
void string::print(int n);
```

8. Write a function that swaps two strings. Use it and `string::strcmp` from the previous exercise to write a program that will sort an array of strings.

9. Use the `vect` type in Section 4.4 in this exercise, and code the following member functions:

```
//adds up all the element values and returns their sum
int vect::sumelem();

//prints all the elements
void vect::print();

//adds two vectors into a third  v(implicit) = v1 + v2
void vect::add(const vect& v1, const vect& v2);

//adds two vectors and returns  v(implicit) + v1
vect vect::add(const vect& v1);
```

10. Write a further constructor for `vect` that accepts an `int` array and its size and constructs a `vect` with these initial values:

```
vect::vect(const int* d, int sz);
```

11. Try to benchmark the speed differences between safe arrays as represented by `class vect` and ordinary integer arrays. Repeatedly run an ordinary element summation routine on `int a[10000]` and one using the `vect a(10000)`. Time your trials.

12. Define the class `multi_v` as follows:

```
class multi_v {
    vect a, b, c;
    int  size;
public:
    int  ub;
    multi_v(int i) : a(i), b(i), c(i) { size = i;
                                        ub = size -1; }
    void assign(int ind, int i, int j, int k);
    void retrieve(int ind, int& i, int& j, int& k);
    void print(int ind) const;
};
```

Write and test code for each member function: `assign`, `retrieve`, and `print`. The function `assign` should assign i, j, and k to a[ind], b[ind], and c[ind], respectively. The function `retrieve` does the inverse of `assign`. The function `print` should print the three values a[ind], b[ind], and c[ind].

13. Use the `list` type in Section 4.6 in this exercise, and code the following member functions:

```
//list a constructor whose initializer is a char array
list::list(const char* c);

//length returns the length of the list
int list::length();

//return the number of elements whose data value is c
int list::count_c(char c);
```

14. Write a member function `append` that will add a list to the rear of the implicit list argument, then clear the appended string by zeroing the head.

```
void list::append(list& e);
```

15. Write a member function `copy` that will copy a list.

```
//the implicit argument ends up a copy of e
void list::copy(const list& e);
```

Be sure you destroy the implicit list before you do the copy.

16. Use the `list` type and add the equivalent five member functions that give you stack functions.

```
reset   push   pop  top_of  empty
```

17. The following function is a traditional C two-dimensional matrix multiply.

```
void mmpy(int a[M][N], int b[N][R], int c[M][R])
{
    int   i, j, k, t;

    for (i = 0; i < M; ++i)
        for (j = 0; j < R; ++j) {
            t = 0;
            for (k = 0; k < N; ++k)
                t += a[i][k] * b[k][j];
            c[i][j] = t;
        }
}
```

Write the corresponding function for class matrix

```
void matrix::mmpy(const matrix& a, const matrix& b);
```

where the result of the multiply is the implicit matrix argument.

18. Construct a three-dimensional safe array type called v_3_d.

```
//Implementation of a three-dimensional safe array
class v_3_d {
    int*** p;
    int     s1, s2, s3;
public:
    int     ub1, ub2, ub3;
    v_3_d(int l1, int l2, int l3);
    ~v_3_d();
    int& element(int i, int j, int k);
    void print();
};
```

Initialize and print a three-dimensional array.

19. We wish to define a C++ class that will resemble sets in Pascal. The underlying representation will be a 32-bit machine word.

```
// Implementation of an ADT for type set.
const unsigned long int masks[32] = {
    0x80000000, 0x40000000, 0x20000000, 0x10000000,
    . . .
    0x80, 0x40, 0x20, 0x10, 0x8, 0x4, 0x2, 0x1};
```

```
class set{
private:
   unsigned long int t;

public:
   set(unsigned long int i) { t = i; }
   set() { t = 0x0; }
   void u_add(int i) { t |= masks[i]; }
   void u_sub(int i) { t  &= ~masks[i]; }
   boolean in(int i)
       { return (boolean)((t  & masks[i]) == masks[i]); }
   void pr_mems() const;
   set set_union(const set& v)
       {set temp; temp.t  = v.t  | t; return(temp); }
};
```

Write the code for `pr_mems` to print out all the elements of the set. Write the code for the member function `intersection` to return the resulting set intersection.

Chapter 5

Operator Overloading and Conversions

This chapter describes operator overloading and conversions of data types. Overloading operators gives them new meanings for ADTs. The ADT can then be used in much the same way as a built-in type. For example, the expression a + b will have different meanings, depending on the types of the variables a and b. The expression could mean string concatenation, complex number addition, or integer addition, depending, respectively, on whether the variables were the ADT string, the ADT complex, or the built-in type int. Mixed type expressions are also possible by defining conversion functions. This chapter also discusses friend functions and how they are crucial to operator overloading.

5.1 The Traditional Conversions

An arithmetic expression such as x + y has both a value and a type. For example, if x and y are both variables of the same type, say int, then x + y is also an int. However, if x and y are of different types, then x + y is a *mixed expression*. Suppose x is a short and y is an int. Then the value of x is converted to an int, and the expression x + y has type int. Note carefully that the value of x as stored in memory is unchanged. It is only a temporary copy of x that is converted during the computation of the value of the expression. Now suppose that both x and y are of type short. Even though x + y is not a mixed expression, automatic conversions again take place; both x and y are promoted to int, and the expression is of type int. The general rules are straightforward.

Automatic conversion in an arithmetic expression x op y

First:

Any char, short, or enum is promoted to int.

Integral values unrepresentable as int are promoted to unsigned.

Second:

If, after the first step, the expression is of mixed type, then, according to the hierarchy of types,

```
int < unsigned < long < unsigned long
    < float < double < long double
```

the operand of lower type is promoted to that of the higher type, and the value of the expression has that type.

To illustrate implicit conversion, we first make the following declarations:

```
char c;       double d;      float f;       int i;
long lg;      short s;       unsigned u;
```

Now we can list a variety of mixed expressions along with their corresponding types:

Expression	Type	Expression	Type
c - s / i	int	u * 3 - i	unsigned
u * 3.0 - i	double	f * 3 - i	float
c + 1	int	3 * s * lg	long
c + 1.0	double	d + s	double

In addition to automatic conversions in mixed expressions, an automatic conversion also can occur across an assignment. For example,

```
d = i
```

causes the value of i, which is an int, to be converted to a double and then assigned to d; double is the type of the expression as a whole. A promotion or widening such as d = i will usually be well behaved, but a narrowing or demotion such as i = d can lose information. Here, the fractional part of d will be discarded. Precisely what happens in each case is machine dependent.

In addition to implicit conversions, which can occur across assignments and in mixed expressions, there are explicit conversions called *casts*. If i is an int, then

```
(double) i
```

will cast the value of i so that the expression has type double. The variable i itself remains unchanged. Casts can be applied to expressions. Some examples are:

```
(char) ('A' + 1.0)
x = (float) ((int) y + 1)
(double) (x = 77)
```

The cast operator (*type*) is a unary operator having the same precedence and right-to-left associativity as other unary operators. Thus the expression

```
(float) i + 3          is equivalent to          ((float) i) + 3
```

because the cast operator (*type*) has higher precedence than +.

These conversions are all found in C. In C++, we also have implicit pointer conversions. As we mentioned in Chapter 4, any pointer type can be converted to a generic pointer of type `void*`. Other pointer conversions include: the name of an array is a pointer to its base element; the null pointer value can be converted to any type; the type function returning T is converted to pointer to function returning T. C++ is generally stricter than traditional C and does not allow mixing of pointer types unless they are correctly cast.

5.2 ADT Conversions

Explicit type conversion of an expression is necessary when either the implicit conversions are not desired or the expression will not otherwise be legal. Traditional C casts are augmented in C++ by a functional notation as a syntactic alternative. C++ has as one aim the integration of user-defined ADTs and built-in types. To achieve this, there is a mechanism for having a member function provide an explicit conversion.

A functional notation of the form

type-name (*expression*)

is equivalent to a cast. The type must be expressible as an identifier. Thus, the two expressions

```
x = float(i);   //C++ functional notation
x = (float) i;
```

are equivalent. The expression

```
p = (int*) q;   //legal cast
```

cannot be directly expressed functionally as

```
p = int*(q);    //illegal
```

However, a `typedef` can be used to achieve this result:

```
typedef  int*  int_ptr;
p = int_ptr(q);
```

Functional notation is the preferred style.

A constructor of one argument is de facto a type conversion from the argument's type to the constructor's class type. In Section 4.3 the string type had a constructor

```
string(const char* p) { len = strlen(p);
                        s = new char[len + 1]; strcpy(s, p); }
```

This is automatically a type transfer from `char*` to `string`. It is available both explicitly and implicitly. Explicitly it is used as a conversion operation in either cast or functional form. Thus

```
string s;
char*  logo = "Geometrics Inc";

s = string(logo);     //performs conversion then assignment
```

and

```
s = logo;             //implicit invocation of conversion
```

both work.

These are conversions from an already defined type to a user-defined type. However, it is not possible for the user to add a constructor to a built-in type such as `int` or `double`. In the string example, one may also want a conversion from `string` to `char*`. This can be done by defining a special conversion function inside the `string` class, as follows:

```
operator char*() { return (s); }   //char* s is a member
```

The general form of such a member function is

```
operator type() { ... }
```

These conversions occur implicitly in assignment expressions, in arguments to functions, and in values returned from functions.

5.3 Overloading and Function Selection

Overloaded functions are an important addition in C++. The overloaded meaning is selected by matching the argument list of the function call to the argument list of the function declaration. When an overloaded function is invoked, the compiler must have a selection algorithm with which to pick the appropriate function. The algorithm that accomplishes this depends on what type conversions are available. A best match must be unique. It must be best on at least one argument and as good on all other arguments as any other match.

The matching algorithm for each argument is as follows:

Overloaded Function Selection Algorithm

1. Use an exact match if found.

2. Try standard type conversions.

3. Try user-defined conversions.

4. Use a match to ellipsis if found.

Let us write an overloaded function `greater` and follow our algorithm for various invocations. In this example, the user type `complex` is available.

```
//overloading functions

#include <iostream.h>
#include <math.h>                 //for sqrt

class complex {
    double real, imag;
public:
    complex(double r) { real = r; imag = 0; }
    void assign(double r, double i) { real = r; imag = i; }
    void print() { cout << real << " + " << imag << "i "; }
    operator double() {return(sqrt(real * real + imag * imag));}
};
```

```
inline int      greater(int i, int j)
                { return ( i > j ? i : j); }
inline double   greater(double x, double y)
                { return ( x > y ? x : y); }
inline complex greater(complex w, complex z)
                { return ( w > z ? w : z); }

main()
{
   int      i = 10, j = 5;
   float    x = 7.0;
   double   y = 14.5;
   complex w(0), z(0), zmax(0);

   w.assign(x, y);
   z.assign(i, j);
   cout << "compare " << i << " and " << j << "  greater is "
        << greater(i, j) << "\n";
   cout << "compare " << x << " and " << y << "  greater is "
        << greater(x, y) << "\n";
   cout << "compare " << y << " and " ;
   z.print();
   cout << "  greater is " << greater(y, double(z)) << "\n";
   zmax = greater(w, z);
   cout << "compare ";
   w.print();
   cout << "  and  ";
   z.print();
   cout << "  greater is  ";
   zmax.print();
   cout << "\n\n";
}
```

The output from this program is:

```
compare 10 and  5  greater is 10
compare 7 and 14.5  greater is 14.5
compare 14.5 and 10 + 5i  greater is 14.5
compare 7 + 14.5i   and   10 + 5i   greater is   7 + 14.5i
```

A variety of conversion rules, both implicit and explicit, are being applied. We explain these in the following dissection.

DISSECTION OF THE *overloading* PROGRAM

```
complex(double r) { real = r; imag = 0; }
```

- This constructor provides a conversion from `double` to `complex`.

```
operator double() {return(sqrt(real * real + imag * imag));}
```

- This member function provides a conversion from `complex` to `double`.

```
inline int     greater(int i, int j)
               { return ( i > j ? i : j); }
inline double  greater(double x, double y)
               { return ( x > y ? x : y); }
inline complex greater(complex w, complex z)
               { return ( w > z ? w : z); }
```

- Three distinct functions are overloaded. The most interesting has `complex` type for its argument list variables and its return type. The conversion member function `operator double` is required to evaluate `w > z`. The `complex` variables `w` and `z` are converted to `double`. Later in this chapter, we shall discuss overloading operators, a construct that will allow us to provide new meanings to existing C++ operators. No conversion is necessary for the return type.

```
w.assign(x, y);
z.assign(i, j);
```

- The first invocation of the member function `assign` requires the `float` argument `x` to be converted to `double`. The `double` argument `y` needs no conversion. The second invocation has both arguments as `int`, requiring conversion. Integer arguments are assignment-compatible with `double`.

```
cout << "compare " << i << " and " << j << "  greater is "
     << greater(i, j) << "\n";
cout << "compare " << x << " and " << y << "  greater is "
     << greater(x, y) << "\n";
```

■ The first statement selects the first definition of `greater` because of the exact match rule. The second statement selects the second definition of `greater` because of the use of a standard widening conversion `float` to `double`. The value of variable x is widened to `double`.

```
cout << "  greater is " << greater(y, double(z)) << "\n";
```

■ The second definition of `greater` is selected because of the exact match rule. The explicit conversion `double(z)` is necessary to avoid ambiguity. The function call

```
greater(y, z);
```

would have two available conversions to achieve a match. The user-defined conversion of `double` to `complex` for the argument y matches the third definition. The user-defined conversion from `complex` to `double` for the argument z matches the second definition. This violates the uniqueness provision for matching when user-specified conversions are involved.

```
zmax = greater(w, z);
```

■ An exact match for definition three.

5.4 Friend Functions

The keyword `friend` is a function specifier. It gives a nonmember function access to the hidden members of the class. Its use is a method of escaping the strict strong typing and data-hiding restrictions of C++. However, we must have a good reason for escaping these restrictions, as they are both important to reliable programming. This feature of the C++ language is controversial.

One reason for using `friend` functions is that some functions need privileged access to more than one class. A second reason is that `friend` functions pass all their arguments through the argument list, and each argument value is subject to assignment-compatible conversions. Conversions would apply to a class variable passed explicitly and would be especially useful in cases of operator overloading, as seen in the next section.

A `friend` function must appear inside the class declaration to which it is a friend. The function is prefaced by the keyword `friend` and can appear in either the public or private part of the class without affecting its meaning. Member functions of one class can be `friend` functions of another class. In this case, they are written in the friend's class using the scope resolution operator to qualify its function name. If all member functions of one class are `friend` functions of a second class, this can be specified by writing `friend class` *class name*.

The following declarations illustrate the syntax:

```
class tweedledee {
   . . .
   friend void alice();              //friend function
   int         cheshire();           //member function
   . . .
};

class tweedledum {
   . . .
   friend int tweedledee::cheshire();
   . . .
};

class tweedledumber {
   . . .
   friend class tweedledee;    //all member functions
                               //of tweedledee have access
   . . .
};
```

Consider the class `matrix` and the class `vect` in Chapter 4. A function multiplying a vector by a matrix as represented by these two classes could be written efficiently if it had access to the private members of both classes. It would be a `friend` function of both classes. In our discussion in Chapter 4, safe access was provided to the elements of `vect` and `matrix` with their respective member function `element`. One could write a function using this access that would multiply without requiring `friend` status. However, the price in functional call overhead and array bounds checking would make such a matrix multiply unnecessarily inefficient.

```
class matrix;                       //forward reference

class vect {
    int*        p;
    int         size;
    friend vect mpy(const vect& v, const matrix& m);
public:
    . . .
};

class matrix {
    int**       p;
    int         s1, s2;
    friend vect mpy(const vect& v, const matrix& m);
public:
    . . .
};

vect mpy(const vect& v, const matrix& m)
{
    if (v.size != m.s1) {       //incorrect sizes
        cerr << "multiply failed - sizes incorrect "
            << v.size << " and " << m.s1 << "\n";
        exit(1);
    }
    //use privileged access to p in both classes
    vect ans(m.s2);
    int   i, j;
    for (i = 0; i <= m.ub2; ++i) {
        ans.p[i] = 0;
        for (j = 0; j <= m.ub1; ++j)
            ans.p[i] += v.p[j] * m.p[j][i];
    }
    return (ans);
}
```

A minor point is the necessity of an empty declaration of the class matrix. This is necessary because the function mpy must appear in both classes, and it uses each class as an argument type.

Friends are controversial because they break through the encapsulating wall surrounding private members of classes. The OOP paradigm is that objects (in C++ these are class variables) should be accessed through their public members. Only member functions should have access to the hidden implementation of the ADT. This is a neat, orderly design principle. The `friend` function, however, straddles this boundary. It is neither fish nor fowl. It has access to private members but is not itself a member function. It can be used to provide quick fixes to code that needs access to the implementation details of a class. But the mechanism is easily abused. However, as in the previous example, some coding situations require its use.

5.5 Overloading Operators

The keyword `operator` is used to define a type conversion member function. It is also used to overload the built-in C++ operators. Just as a function name, such as `print`, can be given a variety of meanings that depend on its arguments, so can an operator, such as +, be given additional meanings. Overloading operators allows infix expressions of both ADTs and built-in types to be written. It is an important notational convenience and in many instances leads to shorter and more readable programs.

The previous section's `mpy` function could have been written as:

```
vect operator* (const vect& v, const matrix& m)
    . . .
```

If this had been done, and if `r` and `s` were `vect` and `t` was a `matrix`, then the natural looking expression

```
r = s * t;
```

would invoke the multiply function. This replaces the functional notation

```
r = mpy(s, t);
```

Although meanings can be added to operators, their associativity and precedence remain the same. For example, the multiplication operator will remain of higher precedence than the add operator. The operator precedence table for C++ is included in Appendix B. Almost all operators can be overloaded. The exceptions are the member operator `.`, the member object selector operator `.*` (see Chapter 8), the ternary conditional expression operator `? :`, the `sizeof` operator, and the scope resolution operator `::`. Furthermore, the autoincrement and autodecrement operators, `++` and `--`, cannot have distinct prefix and postfix meanings (changes in Release 2.1).

Available operators include all the arithmetic, logical, comparison, equality, assignment, and bit operators. The subscript operator `[]` and the function call `()` can also be overloaded. The class pointer operator `->` and the member pointer selector operator `->*` can be overloaded (see Chapter 8). It is also possible to overload `new` and `delete`.

5.6 Unary Operator Overloading

We continue our discussion of operator overloading by demonstrating how to overload unary operators, such as `!`, `++`, `~`, and `[]`. For this purpose, we develop the class `clock`, which can be used to store time as days, hours, minutes, and seconds. We shall develop familiar operations on this `clock`.

```
class clock {
    unsigned long int  tot_secs, secs, mins, hours, days;
public:
    clock(unsigned long int i); //constructor and conversion
    void print();                 //formatted printout
    void tick();                  //add one second
    clock operator ++() { this -> tick(); return(*this); }
};
```

This class overloads the autoincrement operator. The overloaded operator is a member function and can be invoked on its implicit single argument. The member function `tick` adds one second to the implicit argument of the overloaded `++` operator.

```
inline clock::clock(unsigned long int i)
{
    tot_secs = i;
    secs = tot_secs % 60;
    mins = (tot_secs / 60) % 60;
    hours = (tot_secs / 3600) % 24;
    days = tot_secs / 86400;
}

void clock::tick()
{
    clock  temp = clock(++tot_secs);

    secs = temp.secs;
    mins = temp.mins;
    hours = temp.hours;
    days = temp.days;
}
```

The constructor performs the usual conversions from `tot_secs` to days, hours, minutes, and seconds. For example, there are 86,400 seconds in a day, and therefore integer division by this constant gives the whole number of days. The member function `tick` constructs `clock temp`, which adds one second to the total time. The constructor acts as a conversion function that properly updates the time.

The overloaded `operator ++()` also updates the implicit `clock` variable and returns the updated value as well. It could have been coded in the same way as `tick()`, except that the statement

```
return(temp);
```

would be added.

Adding the following code, we can test our functions:

```
void clock::print()
{
    cout << days << " d :" << hours << " h :"
        << mins << " m :" << secs << " s\n";
}

main()
{
    clock t1(59), t2(172799);   //min - 1 sec and 2 days - 1 sec
    cout << "initial times are\n";
    t1.print();
    t2.print();
    ++t1;  ++t2;                   //t1++; t2++ are also possible
    cout << "after one second times are\n";
    t1.print();
    t2.print();
}
```

The output is:

```
initial times are
0 d :0 h :0 m :59 s
1 d :23 h :59 m :59 s
after one second times are
0 d :0 h :1 m :0 s
2 d :0 h :0 m :0 s
```

It would have been possible to overload ++ using a `friend` function as follows:

```
friend clock clock::operator ++(clock& cl)
                  { cl.tick(); return(cl); }
```

Note, since the clock variable must advance by one second, we call it by reference. The decision to choose between a `friend` representation and a member function representation typically depends on whether or not implicit conversion operations are available and desirable. Explicit argument passing, as in `friend` functions, allows the argument to be automatically coerced if necessary and possible.

5.7 Binary Operator Overloading

We continue with our `clock` example and show how to overload binary operators. Basically the same principles hold. When a binary operator is overloaded using a member function, it has as its first argument the implicitly passed class variable and as its second argument the lone argument list parameter. Friend functions or ordinary functions have both arguments specified in the parameter list. Of course ordinary functions cannot access private members.

Let us create an adding operation for type `clock` that will add two values together.

```
class clock {
   . . .
   friend clock operator +(clock c1, clock c2);
};
clock operator +(clock c1, clock c2)
{
   unsigned long int total_sec = c1.tot_secs + c2.tot_secs;
   clock temp = total_sec;
   return (temp);
}
```

Both arguments are specified explicitly. They are both candidates for assignment conversions. The line of code

```
clock temp = total_sec;
```

uses the constructor to convert `total_sec` into a `clock` value. This could have also been written

```
clock temp(total_sec);
```

In contrast, let us overload binary minus with a member function.

```
class clock {
   . . .
   clock operator -(clock c);
};

clock clock::operator -(clock c)
{
   unsigned long int total_sec = tot_secs - c.tot_secs;
   clock temp = total_sec;
   return (temp);
}
```

Remember that there is an implicit first argument. This takes some getting used to.

We shall define a multiplication operation as a binary operation with one argument an `unsigned long int` and the second argument a `clock` variable. The operation will require the use of a `friend` function. A member function must have the first argument from its class.

```
clock operator *(unsigned long int m, clock c)
{
   unsigned long int total_sec = m * c.tot_secs;
   clock temp = total_sec;
   return (temp);
}
```

This requirement forces the multiplication to have a fixed ordering that is type-dependent. To avoid this, it is common practice to write a second over-loaded function:

```
clock operator *(clock c, unsigned long int m)
   . . .
```

5.8 Overloading Assignment and Subscripting Operators

In C++ there are reference declarations. In effect, such type modifiers produce lvalues. On the right side of an assignment expression, an lvalue is automatically dereferenced. On the left side of an assignment expression, it specifies where an appropriate value is to be stored. Both subscripting and assignment make use of these properties of lvalues. For ADTs, we must define such expressions unless satisfactory defaults are available. We shall reimplement the class `vect` from Section 4.4, extending its functionality by applying operator overloading.

The reimplemented class will have several improvements to make it both safer and more useful. A constructor that converts an ordinary integer array to a safe array will be added. This will allow us to develop code using safe arrays and later run the same code efficiently on ordinary arrays. The public data member `ub` has been changed to a member function. This prevents a user from inadvertently introducing a program error by modifying the member. Finally, the subscript operator `[]` is overloaded and replaces the member function `element`.

```
//A safe array type vect with [] overloaded
#include <iostream.h>
#include <stdlib.h>                  //for exit

class vect {
    int* p;                         //base pointer
    int size;                       //number of elements
public:
    //constructors and destructor
    vect();                         //create a size 10 array
    vect(int n);                    //create a size n array
    vect(const vect& v);            //initialization by vect
    vect(const int a[], int n);     //initialization by array
    ~vect() { delete p; }
    //other member functions
    int  ub() { return (size - 1); }  //upper bound
    int& operator [](int i);           //range checked element
};

vect::vect()
{
    size = 10;
    p = new int[size];
}
```

```
vect::vect(int n)
{
   if (n <= 0) {
      cerr << "illegal vect size: " << n << "\n";
      exit(1);
   }
   size = n;
   p = new int[size];
}

vect::vect(const int a[], int n)
{
   if (n <= 0) {
      cerr << "illegal vect size: " << n << "\n";
      exit(1);
   }
   size = n;
   p = new int[size];
   for (int i = 0; i < size; ++i)
      p[i] = a[i];
}

vect::vect(const vect& v)
{
   size = v.size;
   p = new int[size];
   for (int i = 0; i < size; ++i)
      p[i] = v.p[i];
}

int& vect::operator [](int i)
{
   if (i < 0 || i > ub()) {
      cerr << "illegal vect index: " << i << "\n";
      exit(1);
   }
   return (p[i]);
}
```

An overloaded subscript operator can have any return type and any argument list type. However, it is good style to maintain the consistency between a user-defined meaning and standard usage. Thus a most common function prototype is:

class name& operator [] (*integral type*) ;

A reference value is returned in such functions that can be used on either side of an assignment expression.

It is also convenient to be able to assign one array to another. The user can specify the behavior of assignment by overloading it. It is good style to maintain consistency with standard usage. The following member function overloads assignment for `class vect`:

```
vect& vect::operator =(const vect& v)
{
    int s = (size < v.size) ? size : v.size;

    if (v.size != size)
        cerr << "copying different size arrays "
             << size << " and " << v.size << "\n";
    for (int i = 0; i < s; ++i)
        p[i] = v.p[i];
    return (*this);
}
```

DISSECTION OF THE *vect::operator =(const vect& v)* FUNCTION

```
vect& vect::operator =(const vect& v)
```

■ The `operator =` function returns reference to `vect` and has one explicit argument of type reference to `vect`. The first argument of the assignment operator is the implicit argument. The function could have been written to return `void`, but then it would not have allowed multiple assignment.

```
int s = (size < v.size) ? size : v.size;
```

■ The smaller size will be used in the element-by-element assignment. This function will allow a smaller array to have its contents copied into the beginning of a larger array. When assigning from the larger array, it will use only as many elements as are in the smaller array.

```
if (v.size != size)
   cerr << "copying different size arrays "
         << size << " and " << v.size << "\n";
```

■ A warning to the user in case this use was inadvertent.

```
for (int i = 0; i < s; ++i)
   p[i] = v.p[i];
return (*this);
```

■ The explicit argument `v.p[]` will be the right side of the assignment; the implicit argument, as represented by `p[]`, will be the left side of the assignment. The self-referential pointer is dereferenced and passed back as the value of the expression. This allows multiple assignment with right-to-left associativity to be defined.

Expressions of type `vect` can be evaluated by overloading in appropriate ways the various arithmetic operators. As an example, let us overload binary + to mean element-by-element addition of two `vect` variables.

```
vect vect::operator +(const vect& v)
{
    int s = (size < v.size) ? size : v.size;
    vect   sum(s);

    if (v.size != size)
       cerr << "adding different size arrays"
             << size << " and " << v.size << "\n";
    for (int i = 0; i < s; ++i)
       sum.p[i] = p[i] + v.p[i];
    return (sum);
}
```

Now with the class `vect`, as extended, all the following expressions are meaningful:

```
a = b;                     //a, b are type vect
a = b = c;                 //a, b, c are type vect
a = vect(data, DSIZE);     //convert array data[DSIZE]
a = b + a;                 //assignment and addition
a = b + (c = a) + d;       //complicated expression
```

The class `vect` is a full-fledged ADT. It behaves and appears in client code much as any built-in type behaves and appears.

5.9 Turbo C++ Considerations

In older C++ systems, the keyword `overload` was needed to overload functions that were not member functions. This is still available but is considered an anachronism. Turbo C++ implements new rules for the function selection algorithm. These rules are given in simplified form in Section 5.3. A further clarification of these rules with examples are given in this section.

The function argument type list is called its *signature*. The return type is not a part of the signature, but the order of the arguments is crucial.

```
int   sqr(int i);              //signature is int
double  sqr(int i);            //signature is int
void print(int i = 0);         //signature is int
void print(int i, double x);   //signature is int, double
void print(double y, int i);   //signature is double, int
```

In this example, `sqr` is illegally redeclared, but `print` has three distinct signatures. When the `print` function is invoked, the Turbo C++ compiler matches the actual arguments to the different signatures and picks the best match. In general there are three possibilities: a best match, an ambiguous match, and no match. Without a best match, the compiler issues an appropriate syntax error.

```
print(15);          //matches int
print('A');         //converts and matches int
print(9.90);        //converts and matches int
print(str[]);       //no match wrong type
print(15, 9);       //ambiguous
print(15.0, 9);     //matches double, int
print(15, 9.0);     //matches int, double
print(15.0, 9.0);   //ambiguous
print(i, j, k);     //no match too many arguments
print();            //match  int by default
```

There are two parts to the matching algorithm. The first part determines a best match for each argument. The second part sees if there is one function that is a unique best match in each argument. The argument list `15.0, 9.0` has a best match in its first argument to `print(double, int)` and a best match in its second argument to `print(int, double)`. Thus it has no unique best match and is ambiguously overloaded.

For a given argument, a best match is always an exact match. An exact match also includes *trivial conversions*. For type `T` these are:

From	To
//equally good	
T	T
T	T&
T&	T
T	const T
T	volatile T
T[]	T*
//not as good	
T*	const T*
T*	volatile T*
T&	const T&
T&	volatile T&

The first six trivial conversions cannot be used to disambiguate exact matches. The last four are considered worse than the first six. Thus

```
void print( int i );
void print( const int& i );
```

can be unambiguously overloaded.

The simplified rule in Section 5.3 is replaced by a two part rule that distinguishes promotions from other standard conversions. A promotion is going from a narrower type to a wider type. Thus going from `char` to `int` is a promotion. Promotions are better than other standard conversions. Among promotions, conversion from `float` to `double` and conversion using only integral promotion are better than other promotions. Standard conversions also include pointer conversions. These need to be explained in the context of inheritance (see Chapter 6).

It is important to remember that user-defined conversions include constructors of a single argument. This constructor can be implicitly called to perform a conversion from the argument type to its class type. This can happen for assignment conversions, as in the argument matching algorithm. For example,

```
//modify clock from Section 5.6
class clock {
    unsigned long int  tot_secs, secs, mins, hours, days;
public:
    clock(unsigned long int i); //constructor and conversion
    void print();                //formatted printout
    void tick();                 //add one second
    clock operator ++() { this -> tick(); return(*this); }
    void reset(clock& c);
};

    . . .

void clock::reset(clock& c)
{
    tot_secs = c.tot_secs;
    secs = c.secs;
    mins = c.mins;
    hours = c.hours;
    days = c.days;
}

main()
{
    clock c1(900), c2(400);
    . . .
    c1.reset(c2);
    c2.reset(100);
    . . .

}
```

The call to `reset(100)` involves an argument match between `int` and `clock` that is a user-defined conversion invoking the constructor `clock(unsigned)`.

One last piece of advice: Explicitly casting arguments can be both an aid to documentation and a useful way to avoid poorly understood conversion sequences.

Summary

1. Overloading operators gives them new meanings for ADTs. The ADT can then be used in much the same way as a built-in type. For example, the expression a + b will have different meanings depending on the types of the variables a and b. The expression could mean string concat-

enation, complex number addition, or integer addition, depending, respectively, on whether the variables were the ADT `string`, the ADT `complex`, or the built-in type `int`.

2. A functional notation of the form

   type-name (expression)

   is equivalent to a cast. The type must be expressible as an identifier. Thus, the two expressions

   ```
   x = float(i);    //C++ functional notation
   x = (float) i;
   ```

   are equivalent.

3. A constructor of one argument is de facto a type conversion from the argument's type to the constructor's class type. A conversion from a user-specified type to a built-in type can be made by defining a special conversion function. The general form of such a member function is

   ```
   operator type() { ... }
   ```

   These conversions occur implicitly in assignment expressions, in arguments to functions, and in values returned from functions.

4. Overloaded functions are an important addition in C++. The overloaded meaning is selected by matching the argument list of the function call to the argument list of the function declaration. The algorithm that accomplishes this depends on what type conversions are available. A best match must be unique. It must be best on at least one argument and as good on all other arguments as any other match. The matching algorithm for arguments is as follows:

   a. Use an exact match if found.

   b. Try standard type conversions.

   c. Try user-defined conversions.

   d. Use a match to ellipsis if found.

5. The keyword `friend` is a function specifier. It allows a nonmember function access to the hidden members of the class of which it is a friend. Its use is a method of escaping the strict strong typing and data-hiding restrictions of C++.

6. The keyword `operator` is also used to overload the built-in C operators. Just as a function name, such as `print`, can be given a variety of meanings that depend on its arguments, so also can an operator, such as +, be given additional meanings. Overloading operators allows infix expressions of both user types and built-in types to be written. The precedence and associativity remain fixed.

7. Operator overloading typically uses either member functions or friend functions because they both have privileged access. When a unary operator is overloaded using a member function, it has an empty argument list because the single operator argument is the implicit argument. When a binary operator is overloaded using a member function, it has as its first argument the implicitly passed class variable and as its second argument the lone argument list parameter. Friend functions or ordinary functions have both arguments specified in the parameter list.

8. An overloaded subscript operator can have any return type and any argument list type. However, it is good style to maintain the consistency between a user-defined meaning and standard usage. Thus a most common function prototype is:

    class name`& operator [] (`*integral type*`);`

    A reference value is returned in such functions that can be used on either side of an assignment expression.

Exercises

1. The following table has a variety of mixed type expressions. You are to fill in both the type the expression is converted to and its value when well defined.

Declarations and initializations

```
int    i = 3, *p = &i;
char   c = 'b';
float  x = 2.14, *q = &x;
```

Expression	Type	Value
i + c		
x + i		
p + i		
p == & i		
* p - * q		
(int) x + i		

2. For the type `complex`, provide a constructor that converts an `int` to a `complex`. Explain why this is redundant where a constructor from `double` has been provided. Write an explicit conversion that converts `complex` to `double` with the meaning that its value is its real component.

3. If the following line of code from the `greater` program

   ```
   cout << "  greater is " << greater(y, double(z)) << "\n";
   ```

   is replaced by

   ```
   cout << "  greater is " << greater(y, z) << "\n";
   ```

   what goes wrong?

4. Write a function that adds a `vect v` to a `matrix m`. The prototype to be added to `class matrix` and `class vect` is

   ```
   friend vect add(const vect& v, matrix& m);
   ```

   The `vect v` will be added element by element to each row of `m`.

5. The class `complex` as defined in this chapter is:

    ```
    class complex {
        double real, imag;

    public:
        complex(double r) { real = r; imag = 0; }
        void assign(double r, double i) { real = r; imag = i; }
        void print() { cout << real << " + " << imag << "i "; }
        operator double()
                { return(sqrt(real * real + imag * imag));}
    };
    ```

    We wish to augment it by overloading a variety of operators. For example, the member function `print` could be replaced by overloading the ~ operator:

    ```
    void operator ~() { cout << real << " + " << imag << "i "; }
    ```

    Rewrite this as a `friend` function. Also code and test a unary minus operator. It should return a `complex` whose value in each part is negated.

6. For the type `complex`, write the following binary operator functions: add, multiply, and subtract. Each should return `complex`. Write two versions, a `friend` version and a member function version.

7. Write two `friend` functions:

    ```
    friend complex operator +(complex, double);
    friend complex operator +(double, complex);
    ```

    In the absence of a conversion from type `double` to type `complex`, both types are needed in order to allow completely mixed expressions of `complex` and `double`. Explain why writing one with an `int` parameter is unnecessary when these `friend` functions are available.

8. Overload assignment for `complex`. In the presence of the conversion operator for converting `complex` to `double`, what is the effect of assigning a `complex` to `double`?

9. Program a class `vec_complex` that is a safe array type whose element values are `complex`. Overload the operators + and * to mean element-by-element `complex` addition and dot-product of two `complex` vectors, respectively. For added efficiency, you can make the class `vec_complex` a friend of `class complex`.

10. The following member function is a form of *iterator*:

```
int& vect::iterate()
{
    static int i = 0;
    i = i % size;
    return (p[i++]);
}
```

It is called an iterator because it returns each element value of a `vect` in sequence. Use it to write a print function that is not a member function and that writes out all element values of a given `vect`.

11. Exercise 10 has a serious limitation. By providing an iterator that is contained in the class, the element sequencing will not depend on the individual `vect` variable. Thus, if a and b are both `vect` variables, the first call of a.`iterate()` will get the first element of a, and a subsequent call of b.`iterate()` will get the second element of b. So instead we shall define a new class `vect_iterator` as follows:

```
class vect_iterator {
    int   i;
    int *p;
public:
    vect_iterator(vect& v) { p = v.p;  i = 0; }
    int& iterate();
};
```

This class must be a `friend` of `vect`. Write the code for `iterate`. Then for each declaration of a `vect` there will be a corresponding declaration of its iterator. For example,

```
vect a(5), b(10);
vect_iterator it_a(a), it_b(b);
```

Use this to write a function that finds the maximum element value in a `vect`.

12. Define a new class `matrix_iterator` as the iterator that sequences through all elements of a `matrix` (Section 4.7). Use it to find the maximum element in a `matrix`.

13. Redo the string ADT of Section 4.3 by using operator overloading. The member function `assign` should be changed to become `operator=` . The member function `concat` should be changed to become `opera-`

`tor+` . Also, overload `operator[]` to return the `i`th character in the string. If there is no such character, the value –1 is to be returned.

14. Redo the list ADT of Section 4.6 by using operator overloading. The member function `add` should be changed to become `operator+` . The member function `del` should be changed to become `operator--` . Also, overload `operator[]` to return the `i`th element in the list.

15. Modify the class `set` in Chapter 4, Exercise 19, to have overloaded operators +, -, and *.

```
class set{
    . . .
    set operator+(set& v); //define union
    set operator*(set& v); //define intersection
    set operator-(set& v); //define difference
};
```

Test your complete set ADT with the following:

```
main()
{
    set    s(0x5555), t(0x10303021), w, x;

    s.pr_mems(); t.pr_mems(); w.pr_mems(); x.pr_mems();
    w = s + t;          //set union
    x = s * t;          //set intersection
    t = t - s;          //set difference
    s.pr_mems(); t.pr_mems(); w.pr_mems(); x.pr_mems();
}
```

Notice, we now have added a set type that is similar to the built-in Pascal set type.

Chapter 6

Inheritance

This chapter describes inheritance in C++. Inheritance is the mechanism of *deriving* a new class from an old one. That is, the existing class can be added to or altered to create the derived class. Through inheritance, a hierarchy of related ADTs can be created that share code, a feature critical to the ability to reuse code. Inheritance is an important component of OOP (for multiple inheritance, see Chapter 8).

Many useful data structures are variants of one another, and it is frequently tedious to produce the same code for each. A derived class inherits the description of the *base* class. It can then be altered by adding members, overloading existing member functions, and modifying access privileges. The usefulness of this concept can be seen by examining how taxonomic classification compactly summarizes large bodies of knowledge. For example, knowing the concept "mammal" and knowing that an elephant and mouse are both mammals allows our descriptions of them to be considerably more succinct than they would be otherwise. The root concept "mammal" contains the information that mammals are warm-blooded animals and higher vertebrates and that they nourish their young using milk-producing mammary glands. This information is inherited by both the "mouse" and the "elephant," but it is expressed only once: in the root concept. In C++ terms, both "elephant" and "mouse" are derived from the base class "mammal."

C++ supports `virtual` member functions. These are functions declared in the base class and overloaded in a derived class. An ADT hierarchy that is defined by inheritance creates a related set of user types, all of whose objects may be pointed at by a base class pointer. By accessing the `virtual` function through this pointer, C++ selects the appropriate overloaded function at run-time. The object being pointed at must carry around type information so that this distinction can be made dynamically, a feature typical of OOP code. Each object "knows" how it is to be acted on. We briefly touched on this in Section 1.7, and we shall explain it in detail in this chapter.

The OOP design methodology becomes:

1. Decide on an appropriate set of ADTs.

2. Design in their relatedness, and use inheritance to share code.

3. Use virtual functions to process related objects dynamically.

6.1 A Derived Class

A class can be derived from an existing class using the form:

```
class class-name : (public|private) optional base-class-name
{
    member declarations
};
```

As usual, the keyword `class` can be replaced by the keyword `struct`, with the usual implication that members are default `public`. The most complicated aspect of the derived class is the visibility of its inherited members. The keywords `public` and `private` can optionally be used to specify how the base class members are to be accessible to the derived class. We shall explore this in detail in the next section.

An example of deriving a class is:

```
class student {
public:
    int     student_id;
    float gpa;
    char    name[30];
    char    college[15];
    enum    {fresh, soph, junior, senior, grad} year;
    char    major[10];
    void    print();
};

class grad_student : public student {
public:
    enum {ta, ra, fellowship, other} support;
    char dept[10];
    char thesis[80];
    void print();
};
```

In this example, `grad_student` is the derived class, and `student` is the base class. The use of the keyword `public` following the colon in the derived class header means that the public members of `student` are to be public members of `grad_student`.

A derived class is a modification of the base class that inherits the public members of the base class. Thus, in the example of `grad_student`, the `student` members: `student_id`, `gpa`, `name`, `college`, `year`, `major`, and `print` are inherited. Frequently, a derived class adds new members to the existing class members. This is the case with `grad_student`, which has three new data members and a redefined member function `print`. A derived class can also be restrictive. The derived class can change the visibility of members and alter their meanings.

6.2 `public`, `private`, **and** `protected`

The keywords `public`, `private`, and `protected` are available as visibility modifiers for class members. A `public` member is visible throughout its scope. A `private` member is visible to other member functions within its own class. A `protected` member is visible to other member functions within its class and any class immediately derived from it. These visibility modifiers can be used within a class declaration in any order and with any frequency. The usual style is:

```
class foo {
private:  //optional
   . . .
protected:
   . . .
public:
   . . .
};
```

This ordering is from least visible to most visible. In older compilers, where `private` and `protected` are not available, the ordering conforms to the omission of the keyword `private`.

The visibility modifiers can be explicitly used in the class declaration header. If not used there, the default-inherited visibility for `class` is `private`, and for `struct` is `public`. The recommended style is to always be explicit. The most frequent use is to make the base class publicly visible to the derived class. This was seen in the example of `grad_student` in the previous section. In `public` derivation, the derived class inherits both the `public` and `protected` members of the base class and retains these visibilities. Thus a `public` member of the base class is also a public member of the derived class. The `private` members of the base class are not accessible to the derived class. In `private` derivation, the derived class has access to both the `public` and `protected` members of the base class, but within the derived class they are considered `private`.

As can be seen, visibility modifiers in the header can be used to restrict access to members. It is possible to alter this for individual members in the derived class. If a member is transmitted to its derived class as `private`, this can be altered to `public` or `protected`, as in the following:

```
class b {
protected:
   int g;
public:
   int f;
   int h;
   . . .
};

class d : private b {  // f, g, h default to private
protected:
   b::g;    //g is converted to protected
public:
   b::f;    //f is converted to public
   . . .
};
```

In the same manner, a publicly transmitted member can be explicitly converted to `private` or `protected`. Such a declaration is called an *access declaration*. In general, access declarations cannot be used to prevent access to a member accessible in the base class, and they cannot be used to make members visible in the derived class that are inaccessible in the base class. The key design rule is to limit visibility as much as possible, which enhances the modularity of the resulting code. When using classes to implement an ADT, such as a stack, the public code should reflect the operations and functions that client code needs in using the ADT. The implementation details of an ADT, such as the choice of array or list to represent the stack, should be hidden in `private` and `protected` parts of the class.

6.3 A Derived Safe Array Type `vect_bnd`

In this section we develop a safe array type that will be declared with both a lower bound and an upper bound. This style of array declaration was used in Algol 60 and PL/1. It will be derived from the class `vect` found in Section 5.8. The following program implements `class vect_bnd`, which allows safe array declaration using both lower and upper bound specification. It includes a simple test of the class in `main`.

```
//Derived safe array type vect_bnd
#include <iostream.h>

class vect {
   int* p;                     //base pointer
   int  size;                  //number of elements
public:
   //constructors and destructor
   vect();                          //create a size 10 array
   vect(int n);                     //create a size n array
   vect(const vect& v);             //initialization by vect
   vect(const int a[], int n); //initialization by array
   ~vect(){ delete p;}
   //other member functions
   int  ub() { return (size - 1); }    //upper bound
   int& operator [](int i);     //a range checked element
   vect& operator =(const vect& v);
   vect operator +(const vect& v);
};


class vect_bnd : public vect {
   int l_bnd, u_bnd;
public:
   vect_bnd();
   vect_bnd(int, int);
   int& operator[](int);
   int  ub() { return (u_bnd); }
   int  lb() { return (l_bnd); }
};
```

The derived class vect_bnd has its own constructors, which will invoke the base class constructor. There is a special syntax to pass arguments from the derived class constructor back to the base class constructor:

function header : *base-class-name* (*argument list*)

On C++ compilers prior to Release 2.0, the *base-class-name* was optional. Turbo C++ will issue a warning message that the use is obsolete if it is omitted. This syntax is illustrated by the definitions of the derived class constructors.

```
vect_bnd::vect_bnd() : vect(10)
{
    //invokes the constructor vect(10);
    l_bnd = 0;
    u_bnd = 9;
}

vect_bnd::vect_bnd(int lb, int ub) : vect (ub - lb + 1)
{
    //invokes the constructor vect(ub - lb + 1);
    l_bnd = lb;
    u_bnd = ub;
}

int& vect_bnd::operator[](int i)
{
    if (i < l_bnd || u_bnd < i) {
       cerr << "index out of range: " << i << "\n";
       exit(1);
    }
    return (vect::operator[](i - l_bnd));
}

main()
{
    vect_bnd s(-5, 5);

    for (int i = s.lb(); i <= s.ub(); ++i) {
        s[i] = i;
        cout << i << "  ";
    }
    cout << "\n";
}
```

The declaration vect_bnd s(-5, 5) creates a one-dimensional safe array whose lower bound is –5 and whose upper bound is 5, a total of eleven elements. The output from this program is a series of values that is the index sequence of this array:

```
-5  -4  -3  -2  -1  0  1  2  3  4  5
```

DISSECTION OF THE *vect_bnd* CLASS

```
class vect_bnd : public vect {
   int l_bnd, u_bnd;
public:
   vect_bnd();
   vect_bnd(int, int);
   int& operator[](int);
   int  ub() { return (u_bnd); }
   int  lb() { return (l_bnd); }
};
```

■ This is a publicly derived class incorporating the base class `vect`. The class `vect` has as private members the pointer `p` and the `int` variable `size`, which are not directly accessible to `vect_bnd`. They are implementation details that are hidden from clients of this class. The publicly accessible members of `vect` are also publicly accessible members of `vect_bnd`. The identifier `ub` is overloaded. The `operator []` is also overloaded. Selection will depend on type matching unless explicit use of the scope resolution operator is made.

```
vect_bnd::vect_bnd() : vect(10)
{
   l_bnd = 0;
   u_bnd = 9;
}
vect_bnd::vect_bnd(int lb, int ub) : vect(ub - lb + 1)
{
   l_bnd = lb;
   u_bnd = ub;
}
```

■ These are the two different constructors for `vect_bnd`. The first is an empty argument default constructor that creates a ten-element array. The parenthesized expression following the colon in the constructor header is the argument to the constructor for `vect`. The argument `10` is first passed back to the appropriate `vect` constructor and when executed creates a ten-element array. Then the body of this (the derived class) constructor is executed, assigning values to `l_bnd` and `u_bnd`. If a base class has a constructor, it is invoked for the derived class. If the constructor needs an argument list, this is provided in the derived class constructor heading as a parenthesized list following a colon. The second constructor is a two-argument constructor whose arguments are the bound's pair values for the safe array variable. Note how they get used in the implicit argument for the base class constructor.

```
int& vect_bnd::operator[](int i)
{
   if (i < l_bnd || u_bnd < i) {
      cerr << "index out of range: " << i << "\n";
      exit(1);
   }
   return   (vect::operator[](i - l_bnd));
}
```

■ This function will accomplish range-checked indexing into the safe array. Once the index is found to be legal, we wish to return the appropriate element's address. This is an address offset from the base pointer p that is inaccessible to this routine. However, the public member `vect::operator[](int i)` is accessible by use of the scope resolution operator. This base class member does have access to p and can return with the appropriate reference value. If `vect::` were omitted in the `return` statement, the function would be a nonterminating recursion.

6.4 Typing Conversions and Visibility

A publicly derived class is a *subtype* of its base class. A variable of the derived class can in many ways be treated as if it were the base class type. A pointer whose type is pointer to base class can point to objects having the derived class type. This can be confusing since subtle implicit conversions are occurring between base and derived type, and it is sometimes difficult to follow what member is being accessed if the base and derived class overloaded the same member name.

We shall modify our earlier example of `student` and `grad_student`.

```
enum year {fresh, soph, junior, senior, grad};
enum support {ta, ra, fellowship, other};

class student {
protected:
    int     student_id;
    float gpa;
public:
    student(const char* nm, int id, float g)
            { strcpy(name, nm); student_id = id; gpa = g;
            college[0] = '\0'; yr = fresh; major[0] = '\0'; }
    char name[30];
    char college[15];
    year yr;
    char major[10];
    void print();
    void read();
};

class grad_student : public student {
    support s;
public:
    grad_student(const char* nm, support x, int id, float g)
                : student( nm, id, g)
                { s = x; dept[0] = '\0'; thesis[0] = '\0'; }
    char dept[10];
    char thesis[80];
    void print();
    void read();
};
```

The grad_student is a publicly derived type whose base class is student. In the class student, the members student_id and gpa are protected. This makes them visible to the derived class but otherwise treated as private. The class grad_student has one private member s, with all other members public.

Both classes have constructors, and both classes have overloaded read and print as member functions. The constructors act to initialize the non-publicly accessible data members. The constructor for grad_student, as is usual, invokes the constructor for student.

A reference to the derived class may be implicitly converted to a reference to the public base class. For example,

```
grad_student gs("Morris Pohl", ta, 201, 3.2544);
student& rs = &gs;
```

In this case, the variable `rs` is a reference to `student`. The base class of `grad_student` is `student`. Therefore this reference conversion is appropriate.

The `print` and `read` member functions are overloaded. We shall implement the `print` functions and leave as an exercise the coding of the `read` functions.

```
void student::print()
{
    cout << "\n" << name << " , " << student_id << " , "
         << college << " , " << major << " , " << yr
         << " , " << gpa << "\n";
}

void grad_student::print()
{
    student::print();
    cout << dept << " , " << s << "\n" << thesis << "\n";
}
```

For `grad_student::print` to invoke the `student::print` function, the scope-resolved identifier `student::print` must be used. Otherwise, there will be an infinite loop. To see which versions of these functions get called and to demonstrate some of the conversion relationships between base and publicly derived classes, we write a simple test program.

```
//Test pointer conversion rules.
#include "student.h"  //include relevant declarations

main()
{
    student       s1("Mae Pohl", 100, 3.425), *ps;
    grad_student  gs1("Morris Pohl", ta, 200, 3.2564), *pgs;

    ps = &s1;
    strcpy(ps -> college, "Stevenson");
    ps -> yr = fresh;
    strcpy(ps -> major, "Computer");
    ps -> print();
    ps = pgs = &gs1;
    strcpy(ps -> thesis, "Pharmacies as retail outlet.");
    ps -> yr = grad;
    strcpy(pgs -> dept, "Pharmacy");
    ps -> print();
    pgs -> print();     //grad_student::print
}
```

This function declares both class variables and pointers to them. The conversion rule is that a pointer to a publicly derived class may be converted to a pointer to its base class. In our example, the pointer variable `ps` can point at objects of both classes, but the pointer variable `pgs` can point only at objects of type `grad_student`. We wish to study how different pointer assignments affect the invocation of a version of `print`. The first instance of the statement

```
ps -> print();
```

invokes `student::print`. It is pointing at the variable `s1` of the type `student`. The multiple assignment statement

```
ps = pgs = &gs1;
```

has both pointers pointing at an object of type `grad_student`. The assignment to `ps` involves an implicit conversion. The second instance of the statement

```
ps -> print();
```

again invokes `student::print`. The fact that this pointer is pointing at a `grad_student` variable `gs1` is not relevant. The statement

```
pgs -> print();     //grad_student::print
```

invokes `grad_student::print`. The variable `pgs` is of type pointer to `grad_student` and, when invoked with an object of this type, selects a member function from this class.

6.5 Virtual Functions

Overloaded member functions are selected to be invoked by a type matching algorithm that includes having the implicit argument matched to an object of that class type. All of this is known at compile-time and allows the compiler to select the appropriate member directly. As will become apparent, it would be nice to dynamically select at run-time the appropriate member function from among base and derived class functions. The keyword `virtual` is a function specifier that provides such a mechanism, but it may be used only to modify member function declarations.

A virtual function must be executable code. When invoked, its semantics are the same as other functions. In a derived class, its name can be
overloaded, and the function prototype of the derived function must have
matching type. The selection of which function to invoke from among a
group of overloaded virtual functions is dynamic. The typical case is
where a base class has a virtual function and derived classes have their
versions of this function. A pointer to base class can point at either a base
class object or a derived class object. The member function selected will
depend on the class of the object being pointed at, not on the pointer type. In
the absence of a derived type member, the base class virtual function is used
by default.

Consider the following example:

```
//virtual function selection
#include <iostream.h>

class B {
public:
    int   i;
    virtual void print_i() { cout << i << " inside B\n"; }
};

class D1 : public B {
public:
    void print_i() { cout << i << " inside D1\n"; }
};

class D2 : private B {
public:
    D2(){ B::i = 4;}
    int i;
    void print_i() { cout << i << " inside D2 B::i is "
                          << B::i << "\n"; }
};

main()
{
     B    b;
     B*   pb = &b;
     D1   f;
     D2   h;

     h.i = 1 + (f.i = 1 + (b.i = 1));
     pb -> print_i();
     pb = &f;
     pb -> print_i();
     pb = (B*)&h;
     pb -> print_i();
}
```

The output from this program is

```
1 inside B
2 inside D1
3 inside D2 B::i is 4
```

In each case, a different version of `print_i` is executed. Selection depends dynamically on the object being pointed at. This ability to dynamically select a routine appropriate to an object's type is also called *polymorphism*. Different class objects are processed by different functions determined at run-time. Facilities that allow the implementation of ADTs, inheritance, and the ability to process objects dynamically are the essentials of OOP.

The last line of output requires some explanation. The derived class D2 has both a `private` and `public` variable `i`. Its private variable was inherited privately from the base class variable `i`, and it can be accessed by the member function `print_i` using scope resolution. Because D2 is privately derived, it is not a subtype of B, and the cast is required to allow pb to point at h.

Only member functions can be `virtual`. One last restriction: Constructors cannot be `virtual`. Destructors can be `virtual`.

6.6 An Example: A Class Hierarchy

We shall further demonstrate object-oriented programming by modifying the stack implementation of Chapter 4 to store pointers, and a class hierarchy will be used to create various ADTs. In this hierarchy, the base class `proc_data` is the common ancestor of the derived classes. Processing of these varied data types will be dynamic because it will involve a virtual function in the base class.

We begin by showing the hierarchy of derived classes.

```
class proc_data {
public:
    virtual void print() { cout << "virtual\n"; }
};
```

```
struct X {
    int  age;
    char name[20];
};

class X_data : public proc_data {
    X* d;
public:
    X_data(int i, const char* n)
        { d = new X; d -> age = i; strcpy(d -> name, n); }
    ~X_data() { delete d; }
    void print() { cout << d -> name << "  "
                        << d -> age << " yrs "; }
};

struct Y {
    int  salary;
    char name[20];
};

class Y_data : public proc_data {
    Y* d;
public:
    Y_data(int i, const char* n)
        { d = new Y; d -> salary = i; strcpy(d -> name, n); }
    ~Y_data() { delete d; }
    void print() { cout << d -> name
                        << "  $" << d -> salary); }
};

struct Z {
    long int  phone;
    char      state[5];
};

class Z_data : public Y_data {
    Z* z;
public:
    Z_data(int i, const char* n, long int ph, const char* st)
        : Y_data(i, n)
        { z = new Z; z -> phone = ph; strcpy(z -> state, st); }
    ~Z_data() { delete z; }
    void print()
    {
        Y_data::print();
        cout << "  " << z -> phone << " ph "
            << z -> state << "\n";
    }
};
```

The root of this class hierarchy is `proc_data`, which can be used to hold a variety of virtual functions that will be used to process the objects derived from it. This feature leads to a high degree of code sharing and encapsulation. Each class is separately responsible for defining its functionality, and each class can employ routines from an ancestor class.

```
          X_data
        /
proc_data
        \
          Y_data
              \
                Z_data
```

Type hierarchy with base class proc_data

DISSECTION OF THE *proc_data* CLASSES

```
class proc_data {
public:
    virtual void print() { cout << "virtual\n"; }
};
```

■ This class will house all the virtual and default functions. Sometimes, as is the case here, the virtual function is only for diagnostic purposes.

```
struct X {
    int   age;
    char name[20];
};

class X_data : public proc_data {
    X* d;
public:
    X_data(int i, const char* n)
        { d = new X; d -> age = i; strcpy(d -> name, n); }
    ~X_data() { delete d; }
    void print() { cout << d -> name << "  "
                        << d -> age << " yrs" ; }
};
```

■ The derived class X_data manipulates pointers to type struct
  X. A record-keeping system could be gradually developed that
  implemented a variety of such types that could be used to contain,
  access, and operate on different structure types. Our example system will only implement print for these various classes.

```
struct Y {
    . . .
};

class Y_data : public proc_data {
    Y* d;
    . . .
};

struct Z {
    long int   phone;
    char       state[5];
};

class Z_data : public Y_data {
    Z* z;
public:
    Z_data(int i, const char* n, long int ph, const char* st)
        : Y_data(i, n)
        { z = new Z; z -> phone = ph; strcpy(z -> state, st); }
    ~Z_data() { delete z; }
    void print()
    {
        Y_data::print();
        cout << "   " << z -> phone << " ph "
                      << z -> state << "\n";
    }
};
```

■ Class Z_data derives from Y_data, which derives from
  proc_data. The Z_data constructor invokes the Y_data constructor, building an anonymous object of type struct Y. The
  overloaded print invokes its parent's member function
  Y_data::print to process the name and salary information
  before printing phone and state information. Similar code sharing can be distributed throughout this class hierarchy for other
  needed functions.

We next modify the stack type to be a stack of pointers of type
`proc_data*`. Using this pointer type will allow any item of information to
be manipulated dynamically by an overloaded virtual function.

```
typedef proc_data* p_type;
enum boolean {false, true};
enum {EMPTY = -1};

class stack {
   p_type* s;
   int     max_len;
   int     top;
public:
   stack(int size)
      { s = new p_type[size]; max_len = size; top = EMPTY; }
   void    reset() { top = EMPTY; }
   void    push(const p_type& c) { top++; s[top] = c; }
   p_type  pop() { return (s[top--] ); }
   p_type  top_of() { return (s[top] ); }
   boolean empty() { return (boolean)(top == EMPTY; }
   boolean full() { return (boolean)(top == max_len - 1); }
};
```

This modification of an existing class required mostly changes from type
`char` to `p_type`. It is another potent demonstration of the ease with which
such a type system is extended. Objects held in this stack will be manipulated polymorphically by the virtual function `print`.

Let us see how all this works in a simple test.

```
main()
{
   proc_data*  temp[10];
   stack st(10);

   temp[0] = new Y_data(24000, "Sue Hawkins");
   temp[1] = new X_data(18, "Ken Hawkins");
   temp[2] = new Z_data(19990, "Igon Hawkins", 5551110, "CA");

   for (int i = 0; i < 3; ++i)
      st.push(temp[i]);
   for (i = 0; i < 3; ++i) {
      st.pop() -> print();
      cout << "\n";
   }
}
```

The output produced is:

```
Igon Hawkins $19990    5551110 ph     CA

 Ken Hawkins 18 yrs
 Sue Hawkins $24000
```

6.7 A Binary Tree Class

Let us define a generic binary tree class, which shall be used to store generic pointers. Since such a class is not very useful, we shall derive from it a class that can store useful information.

```
//binary search tree

#include <iostream.h>

typedef void   (*pfct)(void*);
typedef void*   p_gen;

class bnode {
   friend  class bstree;
   bnode*  left;
   bnode*  right;
   p_gen   data;
   int     count;
   bnode(p_gen d, bnode* l, bnode* r)
         { data = d; left = l; right = r; count = 1; }
   friend int comp(p_gen a, p_gen b);
   friend void prt(bnode* n);
};

class bstree {
   bnode* root;
public:
   bstree() { root = 0; }
   void insert(p_gen d);
   p_gen find(p_gen d) { return (find(root, d)); }
   p_gen find(bnode* r, p_gen d);
   void apply(pfct f) { traverse(root, f); }
   void traverse(bnode* r, pfct f);
};
```

The individual nodes in this binary tree store a generic pointer data and an int count that will count duplicate entries. The pointer data will match a pointer type in the derived class. The tree will be a binary search tree that will store nodes of smaller value to the left and larger or equal values to the right. We need a method of comparing values that is appropriate to the specific derived type. We use a `friend` function `comp` that is a `friend` of `bnode` and will be coded appropriately for the derived class.

The `insert` function places nodes in a tree, and it must find the position in the tree for the new nodes. The function `p_gen (bnode* r, p_gen d)` searches the subtree rooted at `r` for the information represented by `d`. The overloaded function `p_gen find (p_gen d)` searches the entire tree. The member function `void traverse (bnode* r, pfct f)` walks around the subtree rooted at `r` applying the argument function `f` to each node in turn. This is done for the entire tree by `void apply (pfct f)`.

```
void bstree::insert(p_gen d)
{
    bnode* temp = root;
    bnode* old;

    if (root == 0) {
        root = new bnode(d, 0, 0);
        return;
    }
    while (temp != 0) {
        old = temp;
        if (comp(temp -> data, d) == 0) {
            (temp -> count)++;
            return;
        }
        if (comp(temp -> data, d) > 0)
            temp = temp -> left;
        else
            temp = temp -> right;
    }
    if (comp(old -> data, d) > 0)
        old -> left = new bnode(d, 0, 0);
    else
        old -> right = new bnode(d, 0, 0);
}
```

The `insert` function creates a one-node tree if the tree is initially empty. If the information as represented by the pointer `d` matches existing information as determined by `comp`, then `count` is incremented. Otherwise `comp` navigates through the tree to the appropriate leaf position, where the new node is constructed and attached. Note that the function `comp` can be computationally expensive, and multiple evaluations of it can be eliminated (see Exercise 16).

```
p_gen bstree::find(bnode* r, p_gen d)
{
    if (r == 0)
        return (0);
    else if (comp(r -> data, d) ==  0)
        return (r -> data);
    else if (comp(r -> data, d) > 0)
        return (find( r -> left, d));
    else
        return (find( r -> right, d));
}
```

This is a standard recursion. If the information as pointed at by d is not found, 0 is returned.

The following is also a standard recursion. At each node the formal argument f is applied.

```
void bstree::traverse(bnode* r, pfct f)
{
    if (r != 0) {
        traverse (r -> left, f);
        (*f)(r);
        traverse (r -> right, f);
    }
}
```

We next derive a class capable of storing a pointer to char as its data member.

```
#include "gtree.h"
#include <string.h>

class s_tree : bstree {
public:
    s_tree() {}
    void  insert(char* d) { bstree::insert(p_gen(d)); }
    char* find(char* d)
            { return ((char*)bstree::find(p_gen(d))); }
    void  print() { bstree::apply((pfct)(prt)); }
};
```

The base class insertion function `bstree::insert` takes a generic pointer type as its argument. The derived class insertion function `s_tree::insert` takes a pointer to `char` as its argument. Therefore in the derived class `s_tree`,

```
void  insert(char* d) { bstree::insert(p_gen(d)); }
```

uses the explicit conversion `p_gen(d)`.

We need a function to perform comparison: the promised `friend` function to `class bnode`.

```
int comp(p_gen i, p_gen j)
{
    return (strcmp((char*)i, (char*)j));
}
```

We also show how to use the traversal mechanism to provide a `print` routine for the entire tree. This requires a function of type `pfct` that is applied at each node.

```
void prt(bnode* n)
{
    cout << (char*)n -> data << "\t" ;
    cout << n -> count << "\t";
}
```

There is a good deal more abstraction in the design of `s_tree` than would be the case for a like structure written in C. The payback for this is the ease with which further classes can be derived that utilize the underlying binary tree structure.

6.8 Turbo C++ Considerations

A difficulty in learning C++ are the many distinctions and rules pertaining to the use of functions. We have now completed describing these extensions and shall mention some of these distinctions.

1. A virtual function and its derived instances having the same signature must have the same return type. Other overloaded functions having the same signature can have different return types.

2. Constructors, destructors, and conversion functions do not have return types. The return type of an overloaded `new` operator must be `void*`. The return type of an overloaded `delete` operator must be `void`.

3. All member functions except constructors, friends, and overloaded `new` and `delete` can be `virtual`.

4. Constructors, destructors, overloaded `operator=`, and friends are not inherited.

5. Overloading the operators `=` , `()` , `[]` , and `->` can be done only with member functions. Overloading operators `new` and `delete` can be done only with static member functions. Other overloadable operators can be done with either friend, member, or ordinary functions.

6. A `union` may have constructors and destructors but not virtual functions. A `union` cannot serve as a base class.

Inheritance provides for code reuse. The derived class inherits the base class code. Typically the derived class modifies and extends the base class. Public inheritance also creates a type hierarchy. It allows further generality by providing additional implicit type conversions. It also, at a run-time cost, allows for run-time selection of overloaded virtual functions.

The Project Window

The IDE has a project window that allows the programmer to manage multi-file program development. The project menu is used to create a project file, such as *prog.prj*. This file has a list of program files, header files, object files, and library files that are needed in compiling the program. Proper management of this process allows the programmer to work efficiently on distinct modules without incurring the overhead of constantly compiling the entire program.

Large C++ programs are generally divided into a series of *.h* and *.cpp* files. The header files ending in *.h* are used to contain declarations of related information but typically not code bodies. The code bodies are kept in an associated *.cpp* file. This allows the code to be compiled into an *.obj* file and used without recompilation where necessary by including its corresponding header.

The current standard I/O library used is *iostream.h*. It is an outgrowth of the older stream library *stream.h*. In most cases *iostream.h* is more powerful, and it is compatible with *stream.h* usage. One function that is lacking in *iostream.h* is form(const char* , ...). This allows a printf formatted output style capability. To continue to use this function under Turbo C++, you need to place the appropriate *oldstrmX.lib* in your project file. The *X* can be h (huge), l (large), c (compact), m (medium), s (small), and t (tiny). An example is:

```
//use of form(). This text is form.cpp

#include <stream.h>    //project file has oldstrms.lib
                       //project file has form.cpp

main()
{
   int i, n;

   cout << form("How many integers: ");
   cin  >> n;
   cout << form("Print %d squares and cubes\n", n);
   for (i = 1; i <= n; ++i)
      cout << form("%10d%10d%10d\n", i , i * i, i * i * i);
}
```

Summary

1. Inheritance is the mechanism of *deriving* a new class from an old one. That is, the existing class can be added to or altered to create the derived class. Through inheritance, a hierarchy of related ADTs can be created that share code.

2. A class can be derived from an existing class using the form:

    ```
    class class-name : (public|private)  base-class-name
    {
        member declarations
    };
    ```

    As usual, the keyword class can be replaced by the keyword struct, with the usual implication that members are by default public.

3. The keywords public, private, and protected are available as visibility modifiers for class members. A public member is visible

throughout its scope. A `private` member is visible to other member functions within its own class. A `protected` member is visible to other member functions within its class and any class immediately derived from it. These visibility modifiers can be used within a class declaration in any order and with any frequency.

4. The derived class has its own constructors, which will invoke the base class constructor. There is a special syntax to pass arguments from the derived class constructor back to the base class constructor:

   function header : *base-class-name* (*argument list*)

5. A publicly derived class is a *subtype* of its base class. A variable of the derived class can in many ways be treated as if it were the base class type. A pointer whose type is pointer to base class can point to objects of the publicly derived class type.

6. A reference to the derived class may be implicitly converted to a reference to the public base class. It is possible to declare a reference to a base class and initialize it to a reference to an object of the publicly derived class.

7. The keyword `virtual` is a function specifier that provides a mechanism to dynamically select at run-time the appropriate member function from among base and derived class functions. It may be used only to modify member function declarations. This ability to dynamically select a routine appropriate to an object's type is also called *polymorphism.*

8. Facilities that allow the implementation of ADTs, inheritance, and the ability to process objects dynamically are the essentials of OOP.

Exercises

1. Change the declaration of `grad_student` found in Section 6.1 to

   ```
   class grad_student : student {
   public:
       enum {ta, ra, fellowship, other} support;
       char dept[10];
       char thesis[80];
       void print();
   };
   ```

Explain what goes wrong in the following code:

```
main()
{
   grad_student s;

   strcpy(s.name, "Charles Babbage");
   . . .
}
```

2. The safe array member `vect_bnd::operator[]` in Section 6.3 is guaranteed to be passed a properly indexed element in the `return` statement

```
return (vect::operator[](i - l_bnd));
```

This means that the array index is unnecessarily checked twice. Add an unchecked access function as a member function of class `vect` :

```
int& elem(int i);    //unchecked indexing
```

Use this to modify the `return` statement so as not to recheck the index.

3. Write a member function `print` that prints out a variable of type `vect_bnd`.

4. Write two new constructors for `vect_bnd`:

```
//initialize by vect_bnd
vect_bnd::vect_bnd(const vect_bnd& v);

//initialize by array
vect_bnd::vect_bnd(const int a[], int l, int u);
```

5. Develop a type `matrix_bnd`:

```
class matrix_bnd : public matrix {
   int lb1, lb2, ub1, ub2;
   int size1, size2;
public:
   matrix_bnd(const matrix_bnd& m); //copy existing matrix
   matrix_bnd();                   //5 x 5 matrix
   matrix_bnd(int l1, int u1, int l2, int u2);
   void print();
   . . .
};
```

This is a two-dimensional safe array type that has both upper and lower bounds for each index. Write constructors for this type and a print member function. You should write a member function

```
//reference to an individual element
int& element(int i, int j);
```

that accesses individual elements because overloading `[]` will not work. *Hint*: You can start by modifying the basic `matrix` class in Chapter 5, Exercise 4, or see the `matrix` code in Section 5.7.

6. For `student` and `grad_student` as defined in Section 6.4, code respective input member functions `read` that input data for each data member in their class. Use `student::read` to implement the function `grad_student::read`.

7. Pointer conversions, scope resolution, and explicit casting create a wide selection of possibilities. Using `main` in Section 6.4, which of the following work and what is printed?

```
((grad_student *)ps) -> print();
((student *)pgs) -> print();      //grad_student::print
pgs -> student::print();
ps -> grad_student::print();
```

Print out and explain the results.

8. Modify class `D2` in Section 6.5 to be:

```
class D2 : private B {
public:
   B::i;
   void print_i()
   {
       cout << i << " inside D2 and B::i is "
               << B::i << "\n";
   }
};
```

What is changed in the output from that program?

9. Add a `virtual` function to the class `proc_data` in Section 6.6 called `read` to be used in reading in values to the various data members in the class hierarchy:

```
class proc_data {
public:
   virtual void read() {}
   . . .
};
```

A different member function `read` should be in each of the three classes `X_data`, `Y_data`, and `Z_data`. For example,

```
void X_data::read()
{
   cout << "\nEnter name and age: ";
   cin >> d -> name >> d -> age;
}
```

10. The following uses `class s_tree`:

```
main()
{
   s_tree t;
   char    dat[80], *p;

   cout << "\nEnter strings; exit with an end-of-file\n";
   while ( cin >> dat, cin.good()) {
      p = new char[strlen(dat) + 1];
      strcpy(p, dat);
      t.insert(p);
   }
   t.print();
   cout << "\n\n\n";
}
```

Use this with redirection to produce an ordered count of each string occurrence in a file. The function `cin.good` returns *true* if there is input to read. It is part of the stream input/output library that will be discussed in detail in the next chapter.

11. For `class bstree`, write a destructor. Remember, this must traverse and individually delete nodes.

12. For `class s_tree` write a destructor.

13. The traverse routine as written in this chapter is an *inorder* tree traversal.

```
void bstree::traverse(bnode* r, pfct f)
{
   if (r != 0) {
      traverse (r -> left, f);
      (*f)(r);                         //inorder
      traverse (r -> right, f);
   }
}
```

Run the previous program using both *preorder* and *postorder* traversal. For preorder, the statement `(*f)(r)` goes first, and for postorder it goes last.

14. Develop a class `gen_vect` that is a safe array of generic pointers. Derive a class `s_vect` that is a safe array of `char*`.

15. (Difficult) Using `bstree`, derive a class `itree` that stores a vector of type `int` pointed at by the `data` member of each node. You must write an appropriate `comp` function.

16. Rewrite the code for `bstree::insert` to be more efficient. Do this by assigning the value of `comp(temp -> data, d)` to a temporary variable. This avoids the recomputation of a potentially expensive function call.

Chapter 7

Input/Output

This chapter describes input/output in C++. The software for C++ includes a standard library that contains functions commonly used by the C++ community. The standard input/output library for C, described by the header *stdio.h*, is still available in C++. However, C++ introduces *iostream.h*, which implements its own collection of input/output functions. The header *stream.h* was used on systems before Release 2.0 and is still available under Turbo C++.

The stream I/O is described as a set of classes in *iostream.h*. These classes overload the "put to" and "get from" operators << and >>. Streams can be associated with files, and examples of file processing using streams are given and discussed in this chapter. Much of file processing requires character handling macros that are found in *ctype.h*. These are also discussed here.

In OOP, objects should know how to print themselves, and we have frequently made `print` a member function of a class. Notationally, it is also useful to overload << for user-defined ADTs. In this chapter, we develop output functions for `card` and `deck` that illustrate these techniques.

7.1 The Output Class `ostream`

Output is returned to an object of type `ostream` as described in *iostream.h*. An operator << is overloaded in this class to perform output conversions from standard types. The operator is left associative and returns a value of type `ostream&`. The standard output `ostream` corresponding to `stdout` is `cout`, and the standard output `ostream` corresponding to `stderr` is `cerr`.

The effect of executing a simple output statement such as

```
cout << "x = " << x << "\n";
```

is to print to the screen first a string of four characters followed by an appropriate representation for the output of x followed by a new line. The representation depends on which overloaded version of << is invoked.

The class `ostream` contains public members such as

```
ostream& operator<<(int i);
ostream& operator<<(long i);
ostream& operator<<(double x);
ostream& operator<<(char c);
ostream& operator<<(const char* s);
ostream& put(char c);
ostream& write(const signed char* p, int n);
ostream& write(const unsigned char* p, int n);
```

The member function `put` outputs the character representation of c. The member functions `write` output the string of length n pointed at by p. Since these are member functions, they can be used as follows:

```
int c = 'A';
cout.put(c);        //output A
cout.put(98);       //output b   ascii value 98
cout.put(c + 2);    //output C
char* str = "ABCDEFGHI";
cout.write(str + 2, 3);  //output CDE
```

7.2 Formatted Output and *iomanip.h*

As given, the *put to* operator << produces by default the minimum number of characters needed to represent the output. As a consequence, output can be confusing, as seen in the following example:

```
int  i = 8, j = 9;
cout << i << j ;                    //confused: prints 89
cout << i << "   " << j;           //better: prints 8   9
cout << "i= " << i << " j= " << j; //best:prints i= 8 j= 9
```

Two schemes that we have used to properly space output are either to have strings separating output values or to use \n and \t to create newlines and tabbing, respectively. We can also use *manipulators* in the stream output to control output formatting.

A manipulator is a value or function that has a special effect on the stream it operates on. A simple example of a manipulator is endl defined in *iostream.h*. Its effect is to output a newline followed by flushing the ostream.

```
x = 1;
cout << "x = " << x << endl;
```

This immediately prints the line

```
x = 1
```

Another manipulator flush flushes the ostream, as in

```
cout << "x = " << x << flush;
```

This has almost the same effect as the previous example but would not advance to a newline.

The manipulators dec, hex, and oct can be used to change integer bases. The default base is base ten.

```
//Using different bases in integer I/O.
#include <iostream.h>

main()
{
    int i = 10, j = 16, k = 24;
    cout << i << '\t' << j << '\t' << k << endl;
    cout << oct << i << '\t' << j << '\t' << k << endl;
    cout << hex << i << '\t' << j << '\t' << k << endl;
    cout << "Enter 3 integers, e.g. 11 11 12a" << endl;
    cin >> i >> hex >> j >> k;
    cout << dec << i << '\t' << j << '\t' << k << endl;
}
```

The resulting output is

```
10        16        24
12        20        30
a         10        18
Enter 3 integers, e.g. 11 11 12a
11        17        298
```

The reason the final line of output is 11 followed by 17 is that the second 11 in the input was interpreted as hexadecimal, which is 16 + 1.

The above manipulators are found in *iostream.h*. Other manipulators are found in *iomanip.h*. For example, setw(int width) is a manipulator that changes the default field width to the value of its argument. This value returns after a next argument back to the default. We briefly list the standard manipulators, their function, and where they are defined in the following table.

Manipulator	Function	File
endl	output newline and flush	iostream.h
ends	output null in string	iostream.h
flush	flush the output	iostream.h
dec	use decimal	iostream.h
hex	use hexadecimal	iostream.h
oct	use octal	iostream.h
ws	skip white space on input	iostream.h
setw (*int*)	set field width	iomanip.h
setfill (*int*)	set fill character	iomanip.h
setbase (*int*)	set base format	iomanip.h
setprecision (*int*)	set floating point precision	iomanip.h
setiosflags (*long*)	set format bits	iomanip.h
resetiosflags (*long*)	reset format bits	iomanip.h

7.3 User-Defined Types: Output

User-defined types have been printed by typically creating a member function `print`. Let us use the types `card` and `deck` of Section 5.9 as an example of a simple user-defined type. We write out a set of output routines for displaying cards.

```
//card output

#include  <iostream.h>

char pips_symbol[14] = { '?', 'A', '2', '3', '4', '5', '6',
                         '7', '8', '9', 'T', 'J', 'Q', 'K' };
char suit_symbol[4] = { 'c', 'd', 'h', 's' };

enum suit {clubs, diamonds, hearts, spades};

class pips {
    int  p;
public:
    void assign(int n) { p = n % 13 + 1; }
    void print() { cout << pips_symbol[p]; }
};
```

```
class card {
   int  cd;          //a cd is from 0 to 51
public:
   suit s;
   pips p;
   void assign(int n) { cd = n; s = suit(n / 13); p.assign(n); }
   void pr_card() { p.print(); cout << suit_symbol[s] << "  "; }
};

class deck {
   card d[52];
public:
   void init_deck();
   void shuffle();
   void deal(int, int, card*);
   void pr_deck();
};

void deck::pr_deck()
{
   for (int i = 0; i < 52; ++i) {
      if (i % 13 == 0)            //13 cards to a line
         cout << endl;
      d[i].pr_card();
   }
}
```

Each card will be printed out in two characters. If d is a variable of type deck, then d.pr_deck() will print out the entire deck, 13 cards to a line.

In keeping with the spirit of OOP, it would also be nice to overload << to accomplish the same aims. The operator << has two arguments, an ostream and the ADT, and it must produce an ostream. Let us write these functions for the types card and deck.

```
ostream& operator<<(ostream& out, pips x)
{
   return (out << pips_symbol[x.p]);
}

ostream& operator<<(ostream& out, card cd)
{
   return (out << cd.p << suit_symbol[cd.s] << "  " );
}
```

```
ostream& operator<<(ostream& out, deck x)
{
    for (int i = 0; i < 52; ++i) {
        if (i % 13 == 0)          //13 cards to a line
            out << endl;
        out << x.d[i];
    }
    return (out);
}
```

The functions that operate on `pips` and `deck` need to be friends of the corresponding class because they access private members.

7.4 The Input Class `istream`

Input is returned to an object of type `istream` as described in *stream.h*. An operator >> is overloaded in this class to perform input conversions to standard types. The standard input `istream` corresponding to `stdin` is `cin`.

The effect of executing a simple input statement such as

```
cin >> x >> i;
```

is to read from standard input, normally the keyboard, a value for x and then a value for i. White space is ignored.

The class `istream` contains public members such as

```
istream& operator>>(int& i);
istream& operator>>(long& i);
istream& operator>>(double& x);
istream& operator>>(char& c);
istream& operator>>(char* s);
istream& get(char& c);
istream& get(char* s, int n, int c = '\n');
```

The member function `get(char& c)` inputs, white space characters included, the character representation to c. The member function `get(char* s, int n, int c = '\n')` inputs into the string pointed at by s at most n characters, white space characters included. The optionally specified default character acts as a terminator. If not specified, the input is read up to the next newline. Since this is an ordinary member function, it would be used as follows:

```
cin.get(c);            //one character
cin.get(s, 40);        //length 40 or terminated by '\n'
cin.get(s, 10, '*');   //length 10 or terminated by *
```

When overloading the operator >> to produce input to a user-defined type, the typical form of such a function prototype is:

```
istream& operator>>(istream& p, user-defined type& x)
```

If the function needs access to private members of x, it must be made a friend of its class. A key point is to make x a reference parameter so its value can be modified.

7.5 Files

C systems have stdin, stdout, and stderr as standard files. In addition, systems may define other standard files, such as stdprn and stdaux. Abstractly, a file may be thought of as a stream of characters that are processed sequentially.

Written in C	Name	Remark
stdin	standard input file	connected to the keyboard
stdout	standard output file	connected to the screen
stderr	standard error file	connected to the screen
stdprn	standard printer file	connected to the printer
stdaux	standard auxiliary file	connected to an auxiliary port

The C++ stream input/output ties the first three of these standard files to cin, cout, and cerr, respectively. Typically, C++ ties cprn and caux to their corresponding standard files stdprn and stdaux. There is also clog, which is a buffered version of cerr. Other files can be opened or created by the programmer. We shall show how to do this in the context of writing a program to double-space an existing file into an existing or new file. The file names will be specified on the command line and passed in to argv.

File I/O is handled by including *fstream.h*. This contains classes ofstream and ifstream for output file stream and input file stream creation and manipulation. To properly open and manage an ifstream or ofstream related to a system file, you first declare it with an appropriate constructor. First we study the ifstream behavior:

```
ifstream();
ifstream(const char*, int = ios::in, int prot = filebuf::openprot);
```

The constructor of no arguments creates a variable that will later on be associated with an input file. The constructor of three arguments takes as its first argument the named file. The second argument specifies the file mode. The third argument is for file protection. These are defined as enumerators in class ios as follows:

```
ios::in          //input mode
ios::app         //append mode
ios::out         //output mode
ios::ate         //open and seek to end of file
ios::nocreate    //open but do not create mode
ios::trunc       //discard contents and open
ios::noreplace   //if file exists open fails
```

Thus the default for an ifstream is input mode, and for an ofstream is output mode. If file opening fails, the value 0 is returned.

Let us use this scheme to write a simple file handling program.

```
//dbl_sp: a program to double space a file
//Usage: executable  f1 f2
//f1 must be present and readable
//f2 must be writable if it exists

#include <iostream.h>
#include <fstream.h>
#include <stdlib.h>

void double_space(ifstream& f, ofstream& t)
{
    char   c;

    while (f.get(c)) {
        t.put(c);
        if (c == '\n')
          t.put(c);
    }
}
```

```
main(int argc, char** argv)
{
   if (argc != 3) {
      cout << "\nUsage: " << argv[0]
           << "  infile  outfile\n";
      exit(1);
   }

   ifstream  f_in(argv[1]);
   ofstream  f_out(argv[2]);

   if (!f_in){
      cerr << "cannot open " << argv[1];
      exit(1);
   }
   if (!f_out){
      cerr << "cannot open " << argv[2];
      exit(1);
   }
   double_space(f_in, f_out);
}
```

DISSECTION OF THE *dbl_sp* PROGRAM

```
void double_space(ifstream& f, ofstream& t)
{
   char  c;

   while (f.get(c)) {
      t.put(c);
      if (c == '\n')
         t.put(c);
   }
}
```

■ The get member function gets a character from an ifstream. The put member function puts a character to an ofstream. These functions do not ignore white space characters. The newline character is outputted twice, creating the desired double spacing in the output file.

```
ifstream   f_in(argv[1]);
ofstream   f_out(argv[2]);
```

- The variable f_in is used for input, and the variable f_out is used for output. They are used to create corresponding ifstream and ofstream variables. The corresponding constructors are invoked on the names found in argv[] passed through the command line. If opening the input file succeeds, the ifstream f_in is constructed connected to the file named in argv[1]. If opening the output file succeeds, the ofstream f_out is constructed connected to the file named in argv[2].

```
if (!f_in){
    cerr << "cannot open " << argv[1];
    exit(1);
}
if (!f_out){
    cerr << "cannot open " << argv[2];
    exit(1);
}
```

- If the constructors for either f_in or f_out fail, they return a value of zero, and then an error exit is executed. At this point f_in can be used analogously to cin, and f_out can be used analogously to cout.

```
double_space(f_in, f_out);
```

- The actual double spacing from the input file to the output file occurs here.

Other important member functions that are found in *fstream.h* include:

```
//opens ifstream file
void open(const char*, int = ios::in, int prot = filebuf::openprot);

//opens ofstream file
void open(const char*, int = ios::out, int prot = filebuf::openprot);

void close();
```

These functions can be used to open and close appropriate files. Additional member functions in other I/O classes allow for a full range of file manipulation.

7.6 The Functions and Macros in *ctype.h*

The system provides a standard header file *ctype.h*, which contains a set of macros that are used to test characters and a set of functions that are used to convert characters. This is a standard C header file but is mentioned here because of its usefulness in C++ input/output. Those macros that only test a character return an `int` value that is nonzero (*true*) or zero (*false*). The argument is type `int`.

Macro	Nonzero (true) is returned if:
`isalpha(c)`	`c` is a letter
`isupper(c)`	`c` is an uppercase letter
`islower(c)`	`c` is a lowercase letter
`isdigit(c)`	`c` is a digit
`isxdigit(c)`	`c` is a hexadecimal digit
`isspace(c)`	`c` is a white space character
`isalnum(c)`	`c` is a letter or digit
`ispunct(c)`	`c` is a punctuation character
`isprint(c)`	`c` is a printable character
`iscntrl(c)`	`c` is a control character
`isascii(c)`	`c` is an ASCII code

Other functions provide for the appropriate conversion of a character value. Note carefully that these functions do not change the value of `c` stored in memory.

Function	Effect
`toupper(c)`	changes `c` from lowercase to uppercase
`tolower(c)`	changes `c` from uppercase to lowercase
`toascii(c)`	changes `c` to ASCII code

7.7 Using Stream States

Each stream has an associated state that can be tested. The states are as follows:

```
enum io_state {goodbit, eofbit, failbit, badbit, hardfail};
```

The values for a particular stream can be tested using the following public member functions:

```
int good();  //non-zero if not eof or other error bit set
int eof();   //non-zero if istream eofbit set
int fail();  //non-zero if failbit, badbit, or hardfail set
int bad();   //non-zero if badbit, or hardfail set
int rdstate();  //returns error state
void clear(int i = 0);  //resets error state
```

Applying input/output operations to streams not in the good state leads to a null operation and can cause a program to hang up.

A stream state of *good* means the previous input/output operation worked and the next operation should succeed. A stream state of *eof* means the previous input operation returned an end-of-file condition. A stream state of *fail* means the previous input/output operation failed, but the stream is usable once the error bit is cleared. A stream state of *bad* means the previous input/output operation is invalid, but the stream may be usable once the error condition is corrected. And a stream state of *hardfail* means the previous input/output operation failed irreparably. It is also possible to directly test a stream. It is nonzero if it is either in a *good* or *eof* state.

```
if (cout << x )  //output succeeded
  ...
else
  ...               //output failed
```

The following program counts the number of words coming from the standard input. Normally this would be redirected to use an existing file. It illustrates ideas discussed in this and the last two sections.

```
//A word count program
//Usage: executable < file
#include   <iostream.h>
#include   <ctype.h>

main()
{
    int    word_cnt = 0;
    int    found_next_word();

    while (found_next_word())
        ++word_cnt;
    cout << "word count is " << word_cnt << endl;
}
```

```
int found_next_word()
{
   char   c;
   int    word_sz = 0;

   cin >> c;
   while ( !cin.eof() && !isspace(c)) {
      ++word_sz;
      cin.get(c);
   }
   return (word_sz);
}
```

DISSECTION OF THE *word_cnt* PROGRAM

```
while (found_next_word())
   ++word_cnt;
```

■ The function `found_next_word` attempts to read the next word. It returns a positive word length for each word it finds. If it reads only the end-of-file character, it returns a word length of zero.

```
int found_next_word()
{
   char   c;
   int    word_sz = 0;

   cin >> c;
   while ( !cin.eof() && !isspace(c)) {
      ++word_sz;
      cin.get(c);
   }
   return (word_sz);
}
```

■ A non-white space character is gotten from the input stream and assigned to c. The `while` loop tests that adjacent characters are not white space. The loop terminates when either an end-of-file character or a white space character is found. The word size is returned as zero when the only non-white space character found is the end-of-file. One last point: The loop cannot be rewritten as

```
while ( !cin.eof() && !isspace(c)) {
   ++word_sz;
   cin >> c;
}
```

because this would skip white space.

7.8 Turbo C++ Considerations

We have used *iostream.h* throughout this text. It is perfectly reasonable to want to continue using *stdio.h*. This is the standard in the C community and is well understood. Its disadvantage is that it is not type-safe. Functions like `printf` use unchecked variable length argument lists. Stream I/O requires assignment compatible types as arguments to its functions and overloaded operators. It is also possible that you would want to mix both forms of I/O. When mixed, there are synchronization problems that occur because the two libraries use different buffering strategies. This can be avoided by calling:

```
ios::sync_with_stdio();
```

This is illustrated in the following:

```
//Mix C and C++ I/O.

#include <stdio.h>
#include <iostream.h>

unsigned long fact(int n)
{
   unsigned long f = 1;
   for (int i = 2; i <= n; ++i)
      f *= i;
   return (f);
}
```

```
main()
{
   int n;

   ios::sync_with_stdio();
   do {
      cout << "\nEnter n positive or 0 to halt: ";
      scanf("%d", &n);
      printf("\n fact(%d) = %ld", n, fact(n));
   } while (n > 0);
   cout << "\nend of session" << endl;
}
```

Note that, for integer values greater than 12, the results will overflow.

Turbo C++ also provides a graphics library. To use it, you must include *graphics.h* and link in *graphics.lib*. This can be done by setting the graphics library option. This is toggled in the options menu. A detailed description of these functions and their use is found in the Borland *Library Reference* manual.

Summary

1. C++ introduces *iostream.h*, which implements a wide range of input/output functions, many of which overload the operators << and >>.

2. Output is returned to an object of type `ostream`. An operator << is overloaded in this class to perform output conversions from standard types. The standard output `ostream` corresponding to `stdout` is `cout`, and the standard output `ostream` corresponding to `stderr` is `cerr`.

3. A manipulator is a value or function that has a special effect on the stream it operates on. A simple example of a manipulator is `endl` defined in *iostream.h*. Its effect is to output a newline followed by flushing the ostream.

4. Other manipulators are found in *iomanip.h*. For example, `setw(int width)` is a manipulator that changes the default field width to the value of its argument. This value returns after a next argument back to the default.

5. One can overload << to output user-defined types. The operator << has two arguments: an `ostream` and the user-defined type. It must produce an `ostream`. A typical function that does this is:

    ```
    ostream& operator<<(ostream& out, user-defined type x)
    {
        return (out << ...);
    }
    ```

6. C systems have `stdin`, `stdout`, and `stderr` as standard files. In addition, systems may define other standard files, such as `stdprn` and `stdaux`. Abstractly, a file may be thought of as a stream of characters that are processed sequentially. The standard files are defined in *stdio.h*. The C++ stream input/output ties the first three of these standard files to `cin`, `cout`, and `cerr`, respectively. C++ ties `cprn` and `caux` to their corresponding standard files `stdprn` and `stdaux`. Other files can be opened or created by the programmer.

7. File I/O is handled by including *fstream.h*. This contains classes `ofstream` and `ifstream` for output file stream and input file stream creation and manipulation. To properly open and manage an `ifstream` or `ofstream` related to a system file, you first declare it with an appropriate constructor.

8. File modes are defined as enumerators in class `ios` as follows:

    ```
    ios::in              //input mode
    ios::app             //append mode
    ios::out             //output mode
    ios::ate             //open and seek to end of file
    ios::nocreate        //open but do not create mode
    ios::trunc           //discard contents and open
    ios::noreplace       //if file exists open fails
    ```

    Thus the default for an `ifstream` is input mode, and for an `ofstream` is output mode. If file opening fails, the value 0 is returned.

9. Input is returned to an object of type `istream` as described in *stream.h*. An operator >> is overloaded in this class to perform input conversions to standard types. The standard input `istream` corresponding to `stdin` is `cin`.

10. Each stream has an associated state that can be tested. The states are as follows:

```
enum io_state {goodbit, eofbit, failbit, badbit, hardfail};
```

The values for a particular stream can be tested using the following public member functions:

```
int good();  //non-zero if not eof or other error bit set
int eof();   //non-zero if istream eofbit set
int fail();  //non-zero if failbit, badbit, or hardfail set
int bad();   //non-zero if badbit, or hardfail set
int rdstate(); //returns error state
void clear(int i = 0);  //resets error state
```

Exercises

1. Experiment with your system by defining the following:

    ```
    const long double e = 2.718281828459045235360287471352;
    ```

    Now print this out using:

    ```
    cout << e;
    cout << float(e);
    cout << setprecision(n) << setw(m) << e << endl;
    ```

    In your tests, try several different values for n and m. Remember that floating point precision cannot be exact.

2. See how `float`, `double` and `long double` are stored differently on your machine by repeating the above experiment with e declared as `float` and `double`.

3. Use the manipulators `dec`, `oct`, and `hex` to write out a table that displays 0–255 in each of these representations. Print each value in a field six characters wide. Some sample output follows from our system:

```
dec    oct    hex    chr
  0      0      0
  1      1      1      .
  2      2      2
  .  .  .
 32     40     20
 33     41     21      !
 34     42     22      "
  .  .  .
 65    101     41      A
 66    102     42      B
 67    103     43      C
  .  .  .
253    375     fd
254    376     fe
255    377     ff
```

Explain why the `chr` column does not always print.

4. Exercises 4–6 use the class `clock` from Section 5.6. Overload `<<` to print a standard representation of a `clock` value. Its function prototype should be a friend function of `clock`:

```
friend ostream& operator<<(ostream& out, clock x);
```

5. Write a `clock` member function to produce a string as an output representation of `clock` based on a format. Its prototype is:

```
char* ostring(const char* f);
```

The format string `f` should be broken into four integer formats to be used to format the four data members `secs`, `mins`, `hours`, and `days`.

6. Overload `>>` to read a standard representation of a `clock` value. Its function prototype should be a friend function of `clock`:

```
friend ostream& operator>>(istream& in, clock& x);
```

7. Use the class `complex` from Section 5.3. Overload both `<<` and `>>` to work with `complex` values.

8. Rewrite the *dbl_sp* program so that it gets the name of the input file as a command line argument and writes to `cout`. After this has been done, the command

       dbl_sp infile > outfile

   can be used to double-space whatever is in *infile*, with the output being written into *outfile*.

9. Rewrite the *dbl_sp* program so that it uses a command line option of the form *–n*, where *n* can be 1, 2, or 3. If *n* is 1, then the output should be single-spaced. That is, two or more contiguous newline characters in the input file should be written as a single newline character in the output file. If *n* is 2, then the output file should be strictly double-spaced. That is, one or more contiguous newline characters in the input file should be rewritten as a pair of newline characters in the output file. If *n* is 3, the output file should be strictly triple-spaced. Note, some systems use \r\n (carriage return, newline) to terminate lines.

10. Write a program to number the lines in a file. The input file name should be passed to the program as a command line argument. The program should write to `cout`. Each line in the input file should be written to the output file, with the line number and a space prepended.

11. Write a program that displays a file on the screen 20 lines at a time, with a maximum length of 80 characters per line. The input file should be given as a command line argument. The program should display the next 20 lines after a carriage return has been typed.

12. Modify the previous exercise to display one or more files given as command line arguments. Also, allow a command line option of the form *–n* to be used, where *n* is a positive integer specifying the number of lines that are to be displayed at one time.

13. The value of `cin` and `cout` can be tested to see if I/O operations were successful, as in:

```
if (cin >> n)
   //yes worked ...
else
   //failed
```

Use such a test to ensure that the program for calculating factorials received proper input.

14. We can build additional manipulators by defining functions of the form:

```
ostream& manipulate(ostream& o)
{
    return (o << ...);
}
```

Write such a routine to output two newlines and flush the stream.

Chapter 8

Advanced Features

This chapter describes some advanced features of C++ and recent additions to the language. Many of these changes are described in *The Evolution of C++: 1985 to 1987* by Bjarne Stroustrup (USENIX C++ Papers, Sante Fe, N.M., 1987, pp. 1-21). These changes are incorporated into the Turbo C++ compiler.

Chief among these advanced features is multiple inheritance, which allows a derived class to include inherited members from more than one ancestor class. Pure virtual functions are used to develop *abstract* base classes. Another change is that default assignment and initialization are no longer bitwise copy. These and other advanced topics will be discussed in this chapter. The chapter concludes with an overview of the OOP design process.

8.1 Multiple Inheritance

The examples in the text thus far require only single inheritance; that is, they require that a class be derived from a single base class. This feature can lead to a chain of derivations wherein class B is derived from class A, and class C is derived from class B, ..., and class N is derived from class M. In effect, N ends up being based on A, B, ..., M. This chain must not be circular, however, so a class cannot have itself as an ancestor.

Multiple inheritance allows a derived class to be derived from more than one base class. The syntax of class headers is extended to allow a list of base classes and their privacy designation. An example is:

```
class tools {
  . . .

};
class parts {
  . . .

};
class labor {
  . . .

};
class plans : public tools, public parts, public labor {
  . . .

};
```

In this example, the derived class `plans` publicly inherits the members of all three base classes. This parental relationship is described by the inheritance *directed acyclic graph* (DAG). The DAG is a graph structure whose nodes are classes and whose directed edges point from base to derived class. To be legal it cannot be circular, so no class may, through its inheritance chain, inherit from itself.

In deriving an identically named member from different classes, ambiguities may arise. These derivations are allowed, provided the user does not make an ambiguous reference to such a member. For example,

```
class tools {
public:
    int cost();
    . . .
};

class labor {
public:
    int cost();
    . . .
};

class parts {
public:
    int cost();
    . . .
};

class plans : public tools, public parts, public labor {
public:
    int tot_cost() { return (parts::cost() + labor::cost()); }
    . . .
};

int foo()
{
    int   price;
    plans* ptr;

    price = ptr -> cost();
    . . .
}
```

In the body of `foo`, the reference to `cost` is inherently ambiguous. It can be resolved by either properly qualifying `cost` using the scope resolution operator or adding a member `cost` to the derived class `plans`.

One further modification to the original inheritance scheme has been made: `virtual` inheritance. With multiple inheritance, two base classes can be derived from a common ancestor. If both base classes are used in the ordinary way by their derived class, that class will have two subobjects of the common ancestor. This duplication, if not desirable, can be eliminated by using `virtual` inheritance. An example is:

```
class under_grad : public virtual student {
    . . .
};
```

```
class grad : public virtual student {
   . . .

};

class department : public under_grad, public grad {
   . . .

};
```

Without the use of `virtual` in this example, `class department` would have objects of `class::under_grad::student` and also objects of class `class::grad::student`.

The early releases of C++ left unspecified the order of execution for initializing constructors in base and member constructors. Most of the time these constructions were independent of each other, and the results were independent of order. With the addition of multiple inheritance, however, it became unnecessarily hazardous to continue this laxness. Thus the current ordering is:

1. Explicit reference to base class constructors in the order in which they are listed after the header colon.

2. Unmentioned base classes in the order in which they are declared.

3. Explicit reference to member class constructors in the order in which they are listed after the header colon.

Virtual base classes have special precedence and are constructed before any of their derived classes. They are constructed before any nonvirtual base classes. Their construction order depends on their DAG. It is a depth-first, left-to-right order. Destructors are invoked in reverse order of constructors. These rules, although complicated, should conform to one's intuition, and a client program's correctness should not depend on constructor/destructor ordering.

A further improvement is that the class name is used for each base class initializer. The old style of just using a parenthesized argument list that implicitly called the base class constructor is allowed for single inheritance, but it is poor style even for that case. Finally, the associated destructors are called in the reverse order from constructor invocation.

Let us illustrate by elaborating on a previous example.

```
class tools {
   . . .
public:
   tools(char*);
   ~tools();
   . . .
};

class parts {
   . . .
public:
   parts(char*);
   ~parts();
   . . .
};

class labor {
   . . .
public:
   labor(int);
   ~labor();
   . . .
};

class plans : public tools, public parts, public labor {
   . . .
   special a;   //member class with constructor
public:
   plans(int m) : labor(m), tools("lathe"), a(m), parts("widget")
      { . . . }
   ~plans();
   . . .
};
```

In this case, the member constructor a(m) appears before the base class constructor parts("widget") but by our rules is invoked last. Since its constructor was last, its destructor is invoked first, followed by ~parts, ~tools, ~labor, and ~plans.

For a concrete worked-out example of multiple inheritance, look at *iostream.h*. This contains the class iostream, which is derived from istream and ostream.

8.2 Abstract Base Classes

A type hierarchy usually has its root class contain a number of virtual functions. Virtual functions provide for dynamic typing (see Section 6.5). Often these virtual functions in the root class are dummy functions. They have an empty body in the root class, but they will be given specific meanings in the derived classes. In Turbo C++, the *pure virtual function* is introduced for this purpose. A pure virtual function is a virtual member function whose body is undefined. Notationally it is declared inside the class as follows:

```
virtual function prototype = 0;
```

A derived class must define or declare each pure virtual function in its immediate base class.

A class that has at least one *pure virtual* function is an *abstract class*. It is useful to have a root class for a type hierarchy be an *abstract class*. It would have the basic common properties of its derived classes but would not itself be used to declare objects.

We want to design an object-oriented data base (see Section 6.6). The data base will be built up from a type hierarchy that will have different objects whose root class will be the abstract class object.

```
class data {
      //abstract class - root of type hierarchy
public:
   virtual void print() = 0;
};

class person : public virtual data {
protected:
   char      f_name[10], l_name[20];
   int       age;
   long int  soc_sec;
public:
   person();
   person(const char* fn, const char* ln, int a, long int ss);
   void print();
};
```

```
class object {
protected:
   data*   record;
   int     key;
public:
   virtual void print() = 0;
   virtual void del(int k) = 0;
   virtual void insert(const data* ) = 0;
   int     display_key() { return key; }
};

class read_object : public object {
public:
   void print();
   void del(int k)   //k unused but signature must match
      { cerr << "\nError: Attempt to delete read-only data"; }
   void insert(const data* d);
};
```

The two classes `data` and `object` are abstract base classes. It would be illegal to declare objects of these types. The class `data` serves as the base class for a type hierarchy that defines the different forms of data objects used in our program. Notice how easy it is to extend this scheme to new forms of data. The class `object` is an abstract base class used to derive different types of database objects.

Virtual derivation was used in `class person`. This use anticipates the use of multiple inheritance at a later point in the development of this database program. A new derived class from `data` could be a combination of several existing derived classes. A final point: The return type of virtual functions is restricted to be the same in all derived classes. This is a natural restriction since otherwise expression evaluation involving virtuals would have to be dynamic.

8.3 Default Assignment and Overloading new

In Chapter 5 we discussed overloading the assignment operator. If this operator were not overloaded for a particular user type, then assignment between two objects of that type, for early C++ compilers, was bitwise copy. Current systems default to a more sophisticated member-by-member assignment. This rule is recursive until components that are built-in types are assigned in the usual way.

This rule is safer than the original bitwise copy method. In instances where a class, call it A, had a data member of a different class, call it B, and B had assignment overloaded and A did not, there was a possibility of errors if objects of type A were bitwise copy-assigned.

The same idea applies to default initializations. The user in most cases need not have a constructor of type X(X&) for class X. The compiler is responsible for providing both assignment and initialization based on the recursive member-by-member subassignment rule. Of course, where necessary, the user can still overload these member functions to produce a different result.

A further change allows the operators `new` and `delete` to be overloaded. This feature provides a simple mechanism for user-defined manipulation of free store. Older methods for directly controlling allocation involved the explicit manipulation of the `this` pointer. For example:

```
class X {
   . . .
public:
   void* operator new(unsigned size) { return (malloc(size)); }
   void  operator delete(X* ptr) { free((void*)ptr); }
   X(unsigned size) { new(size); }
   ~X() { delete(this); }
   . . .
};
```

8.4 Pointer Operators

The structure pointer operator `->` can be overloaded as a nonstatic class member function. (This restriction also applies to the assignment operator, the subscript operator, and the function call operator.) The overloaded structure pointer operator is a unary operator on its left operand. The argument must be either a class object or a reference of this type. It can return either pointer to a class object or an object of a class for which `operator ->` is defined.

In the following example, we overload the structure pointer operator inside the class `t_ptr`. Objects of type `t_ptr` act as controlled access pointers to objects of type `triple`.

```
// Overloading the structure pointer operator.
#include <iostream.h>
enum boolean {false, true};

class triple {
private:
    int       i, j, k;
public:
    triple(int a, int b, int c) { i = a; j = b; k = c; }
    void print() { cout << "\ni = " << i
                        << ", j = " << j << ", k = " << k; }
};

triple    unauthor(0, 0, 0);

class t_ptr {
    boolean   access;
    triple*   ptr;
public:
    t_ptr(boolean f, triple* p) { access = f; ptr = p; }
    triple*   operator ->() ;
};

triple* t_ptr::operator ->()
{
    if (access)
        return (ptr);
    else {
        cout << "\nunauthorized access";
        return (&unauthor);
    }
}
```

The variable `t_ptr::access` is tested by the overloaded `operator ->`, and, if `true`, access is granted. The following code tests this:

```
main()
{
    triple  a(1, 2, 3), b(4, 5, 6);
    t_ptr ta(false, &a), tb(true, &b);
    ta -> print();   //access denied
    tb -> print();   //access granted
}
```

Pointer to Class Member

A pointer to class member is *distinct* from a pointer to class. A pointer to class member's type is $T::*$, where T is the class name. C++ has two operators that act to dereference a pointer to class member. The pointer to member operators are:

```
.*
->*
```

Think of *obj.*ptr_mem* as first dereferencing the pointer to obtain a member variable and then accessing the member for the designated *obj*. The following code shows how to use these operators:

```
//Pointer to class member.

#include <iostream.h>

class X {
private:
    int   hide;
public:
    int   visible;
    void print()
        { cout << "\nhide = " << hide
               << " visible = " << visible; }
    void reset() { visible = hide; }
    void set(int i) { hide = i; }
};

typedef void (X::*pfcn)();

main()
{
    X    a, b, *pb = &b;
    int X::*pXint = &X::visible;
    pfcn pF = &X::print;

    a.set(8); a.reset();
    b.set(4); b.reset();
    a.print();
    a.*pXint += 1;
    a.print();
    cout << "\nb.visible = " << pb ->*pXint;
    (b.*pF)();
    pF = &X::reset;
    (a.*pF)();
    a.print();
    cout << "\n";
}
```

DISSECTION OF THE *ptr_mem* PROGRAM

```
typedef void (X::*pfcn)();
```

■ This says that `pfcn` is pointer to class `X` member whose base type is a function of no arguments returning `void`. Member functions `X::print` and `X::reset` match this type.

```
int X::*pXint = &X::visible;
pfcn pF = &X::print;
```

■ This declares `pXint` to be a pointer to class `X` member whose base type is `int`. It is initialized to point at the member `X::visible`. The pointer `pF` is initialized to point at the member function `X::print`.

```
a.*pXint += 1;
```

■ This is equivalent to `++a.visible`.

```
cout << "\nb.visible = " << pb ->*pXint;
(b.*pF)();
```

■ The pointer expression is equivalent to `pb -> visible`. The function call is equivalent to `b.print()`.

```
pF = &X::reset;
(a.*pF)();
```

■ The pointer `pf` is assigned the address of `X::reset`. The function call is equivalent to `a.reset()`.

8.5 Scope and Linkage

Large C programs are partitioned into multifile units that can be compiled separately. Linking such separate modules requires resolving external references. In C, the rules for resolving external references are frequently system-dependent.

In C++, these rules are explicit. The key difference is that external non-static variables must be defined in exactly one place. As usual, `static` `extern` constructs can be defined in multiple files because they are local to a given file. Use of the keyword `extern` together with an initializer constitutes defining a variable. Using the keyword `extern` without an initializer constitutes a declaration but not a definition. The following examples illustrate these rules. The first example is legal.

```
//file prog1.c
   char   c;            //definition of c
   . . .

//file prog2.c
   extern char c;       //declaration of c
   . . .
```

The second example is illegal.

```
//file prog1.c
   char    c;
   double x = 0.9;
   . . .

//file prog2.c
   char          c;          //illegal second definition
   extern int    x;          //illegal type mismatch
   extern int    k;          //illegal no declaration
   . . .
```

These two files have three errors. Most C compilers would complain only about the type mismatch. The third error has the variable k defined but not declared.

Constant and `inline` declarations at file scope that are not explicitly declared `extern` are local to the file. If these names are to be used in other files, they need to be imported there using the preprocessor directive `include`.

```
//file my_stuff.h
   const double pi = 3.14159;
   inline   double max(double a, double b)
         { return (a < b) ? b : a); }
   . . .

//file main_prog.c
#include <my_stuff.h>
   . . .
```

In general, it is good style to avoid reliance on the `#define` mechanism to produce simple constants and macros. Macro expansion occurs as string replacement and leads to subtle errors in the source code. For particular applications, it is desirable to place related definitions into header files. Good examples of this are found in the system header files, such as `iostream.h`.

Linkage rules for non-C++ functions can be specified using a *linkage-specification*. Some examples are:

```
extern "C" atoi(const char* nptr);   //C linkage

extern "C" {
#include <stdio.h>
}                       //C linkage for these prototypes

extern "Pascal" {
   sin(double);
   cos(double);
   tan(double);
}                       //Pascal linkage if available
```

This specification is at file scope and is system-dependent as to which languages are supported.

8.6 Iterators

Iterators were mentioned briefly in Exercises 5.10 and 5.11. An iterator is a mechanism for accessing all components of a given type. The `for` statement provides a built-in iterator for simple arrays. Classes allow data to be hidden from general access, and, typically, an iterator needs to be either a member function or a friend function of the class. The following example shows an iterator class associated with a safe vector class that provides ordered access to all elements:

```
//iterators : vector class

class  vector {
   friend class vector_iterator;
   int* v;
   int  sz;
```

```
public:
    vector(int);
    ~vector() { delete v; }

    int  size()  { return (sz); }
    int& operator[](int);
};

class  vector_iterator {
    int      cur_ind;
    vector* bv;
public:
    vector_iterator(vector& v) { bv = &v; cur_ind = 0; }
    int& next();
};
```

The iterator class `vector_iterator` has two private data members, both typical of such classes. The variable `cur_ind` is used to keep track of the ordering of element presentation. It is an index. The pointer variable `bv` is the reference to the associated vector variable. The constructor initializes these hidden variables. The member function `next` accesses each element in turn using `cur_ind` as its internal protected index into a variable of class `vector`.

The member function `next` is written as follows:

```
int& vector_iterator::next()
{
    if (cur_ind < bv -> sz)
        return (bv -> v[cur_ind++]);
    else {
        cur_ind = 0;
        return (bv -> v[cur_ind++]);
    }
}
```

This member function accesses private members of `class vector` and must be a friend of that class. The pointer variable `bv` is bound to an instance of `class vector`. The index variable `cur_ind` is autoincremented each time `next` is called and is tested to make certain it does not exceed the internal `vector` element bound `sz`. It wraps around to 0 whenever it gets to this limit.

The following example shows how to use the iterator class to output the individual elements of a `vector` and contrasts this scheme with a traditional iteration:

```
ostream& operator<<(ostream& s, vector& w)
{
    s << "\nVECTOR  0 to " << w.size() - 1 << endl;
    for (int i = 0; i < w.size(); ++i)
        s << setw(8) << w[i];
    s << endl;
    return (s);
}
```

This is a standard style for overloading the iostream operator << to output
a variable of type vector. A traditional for loop is used to access elements
of vector using public member functions. Now we write a main function
to output two vector variables:

```
main()
{
    vector             u(25), w(10);
    vector_iterator   w_it(w);

    for (int i = 0; i < u.size(); ++i)
        u[i] = i;
    cout << u;

    for (i = 0; i < w.size(); ++i)
        cout << (w_it.next() = 2 * i) << "\t";
}
```

The first for loop is traditional C. It initializes the vector u. The second
for loop uses the iterator function next to initialize and print out consecu-
tive values of the associated vector w.

8.7 An Example: Word Frequency

In this section we develop a multifile program using header files. The program will count the frequency of occurrence of words in a specified file and
will output an alphabetized list with each word's frequency.

Part of our purpose is to show how C++ allows you to write programs
quickly and modularly. We shall reuse previously developed code. The
binary search tree, which was discussed in Chapter 6, is a convenient and
efficient means of storing this information.

```
//file bstree.h  binary search tree

typedef void (*pfct)(void*);
typedef void*  p_gen;

class bnode {
   friend class bstree;
   bnode* left;
   bnode* right;
   p_gen  data;
   int    count;
   bnode(p_gen d, bnode* l, bnode* r)
       { data = d; left = l; right = r; count = 1; }
   friend int comp(p_gen a, p_gen b);
   friend void prt(bnode* n);
};

class bstree {
   bnode* root;
public:
   bstree() { root = 0; }
   void   insert(p_gen d);
   p_gen find(p_gen d) { return (find(root, d)); }
   p_gen find(bnode* r, p_gen d);
   void   apply(pfct f) { traverse(root, f); }
   void   traverse(bnode* r, pfct f);
};
```

The class bstree is capable of storing a generic pointer and a count at each node of a binary search tree. It is a prototype class from which other classes are derived as needed.

```
//file stree.h

void prt(bnode* n);

int comp(p_gen i, p_gen j);

class s_tree : bstree {
public:
   s_tree() {}
   void   insert(char* d) { bstree::insert(p_gen(d)); }
   char* find(char* d)
      { return ((char* )bstree::find(p_gen(d))); }
   void   print() { bstree::apply((pfct)prt); }
};
```

The class s_tree uses the insert function to store a pointer to char. In effect, each node will store a string. Each new word will be inserted as a string into the s_tree. The code for implementing these classes is stored in corresponding *.c files in order to allow separate compilation.

```
//file bstree.c
#include "bstree.h"

void bstree::insert(p_gen d)
{
    bnode* temp = root;
    bnode* old;

    if (root == 0) {
        root = new bnode(d, 0, 0);
        return;
    }
    while (temp != 0) {
        old = temp;
        if (comp(temp -> data, d) == 0) {
            (temp -> count)++;
            return;
        }
        if (comp(temp -> data, d) > 0)
            temp = temp -> left;
        else
            temp = temp -> right;
    }
    if (comp(old -> data, d) > 0)
        old -> left = new bnode(d, 0, 0);
    else
        old -> right = new bnode(d, 0, 0);
}

p_gen bstree::find(bnode* r, p_gen d)
 {
    if (r == 0)
        return (0);
    else if (comp(r -> data, d) == comp(d, r -> data))
        return (r -> data);
    else if (comp(r -> data, d))
        return (find( r -> left, d));
    else
        return (find( r -> right, d));
 }
```

```
void bstree::traverse(bnode* r, pfct f)
{
   if (r != 0) {
       traverse (r -> left, f);
       (*f)(r);
       traverse (r -> right, f);
   }
}
```

We have already discussed this code in Chapter 6.

```
//stree.c

#include "bstree.h"
#include "stree.h"
#include <string.h>
#include <iostream.h>

void prt(bnode* n)
{
   cout << (char*)n -> data << "\t" ;
   cout << n -> count << "\t";
}

int comp(p_gen i, p_gen j)
{
   return (strcmp((char*)i, (char*)j));
}
```

The various *.h files are necessary to provide appropriate definitions for these two functions. For example, strcmp is defined in *string.h,* and cout is defined in *iostream.h.* The prt function prints out a word and its frequency of occurrence as stored in count. The comp function lexicographically compares two strings. It is used for insertion into the binary search tree.

The next header file describes the function and constants related to extracting individual words from an ifstream:

```
//get_word.h

#include <ctype.h>
#include <fstream.h>
enum boolean {false, true};
const maxlen = 80;
boolean get_word(char*, ifstream&);
```

Its corresponding *.c file is:

```
#include "get_word.h"

boolean  get_word(char* word_buf, ifstream& in)
{
    char   c;
    int    len = 0;

    while(in.get(c), !isalpha(c) && in.good())
        ;
    if (!in.good())
        return (false);
    else {
        word_buf[len++] = (isupper(c) ? tolower(c) : c);
        while (in.get(c), isalpha(c) && in.good())
            if (len < maxlen)
                word_buf[len++] = (isupper(c) ? tolower(c) : c);
        word_buf[len] = '\0';
        return (true);
    }
}
```

DISSECTION OF THE *get_word* FUNCTION

```
#include "get_word.h"
```

■ This is the header file needed by this code. By separately compiling this code into an object file—for example, *get_word.o*—this routine can be conveniently used by any file that includes its header.

```
boolean  get_word(char* word_buf, ifstream& in)
```

■ The input will be taken from an `ifstream`. The output will be a single word. If input fails, then `false` is returned; if a word is found, then `true` is returned.

```
while(in.get(c), !isalpha(c) && in.good())
    ;
```

■ The loop continues until an alphabetic character is detected. We use a comma expression. First a character is read into c; then it is tested. The loop also detects an end-of-file or an input failure.

```
if (!in.good())
   return (false);
```

■ This indicates an input failure, normally an end-of-file.

```
word_buf[len++] = (isupper(c) ? tolower(c) : c);
while (in.get(c), isalpha(c) && in.good())
   if (len < maxlen)
      word_buf[len++] = (isupper(c) ? tolower(c) : c);
word_buf[len] = '\0';
return (true);
```

■ This is the loop that collects the alphabetic characters into
  word_buf. A conversion to lowercase is made on all letters.

What remains is to put this all together into main.

```
//main for producing word frequencies
//Usage: executable   f1
//f1 must be present and readable
//An alphabetized word list is read to cout
//with frequency counts of all words in f1.

#include "bstree.h"
#include "stree.h"
#include "get_word.h"
#include <string.h>
#include <stdlib.h>

main(int argc, char** argv)
{
   if (argc != 2) {
      cout << "\nUsage:" << argv[0] << "  infile\n";
      exit(1);
   }

   ifstream f_in(argv[1]); //open input file

   if (!f_in) {
      cerr << "cannot open " << argv[1];
      exit(1);
   }
```

```
    s_tree    t;
    char      dat[80];
    char*     p;

    while (get_word(dat, f_in)) {
        p = new char[strlen(dat) + 1];
        strcpy(p, dat);
        t.insert(p);
    }
    t.print();
    cout << "\n\n\n";
}
```

The `main` function opens the input file for reading. It gets each word and stores it temporarily into `dat`. It stores the word permanently in a string created by `new`. This string is inserted into the search tree `t`. Finally, `t.print()` outputs the alphabetized word frequencies. Each piece of the code can be compiled separately.

8.8 OOP: Object-Oriented Programming

The central feature of OOP is its encapsulation of an appropriate set of data types and their operations. The class, with its member functions and operator overloading, provides an appropriate coding tool. An object in this formulation is an instance of a class—in other words, a class variable or constant. Classes allow for the implementation of abstract data types.

A second feature is its promotion of code reuse through the inheritance mechanism. Without this reuse mechanism, each minor variation of an ADT would require code replication. Inheritance gives the programmer the ability to build a type hierarchy suitable to a particular problem domain.

A third feature is dynamic binding of types. The `virtual` function provides the ability to bind type at run-time. Thus an object determines how it is acted on. For example, let `shape` be a base class and `draw` and `area` be virtual functions in `shape`. Assume that there is a set of derived classes, such as `rectangle`, `circle`, `pentagon`, and `triangle` and that each can know how to draw itself or compute its own area. A pointer to type `shape` can be used to dynamically process objects of any of the `shape` subtypes. Code for drawing shapes is more easily maintained because it is highly modular. New `shape` types can readily be added to with inheritance.

A fourth feature is data hiding. Access privileges can be managed and limited to whatever group of functions truly needs access to implementation details. The visibility modifiers `public`, `protected`, and `private` control client access to objects. This control promotes modularity and robustness.

The OOP programming task can be more difficult than normal procedural programming as found in C or Pascal. There is, for example, at least one extra design step before one gets to the coding of algorithms. This extra step involves the hierarchy of types that is useful for the problem at hand. Frequently, one solves a problem more generally than is strictly necessary.

The extra step pays dividends in several ways. The solution is more encapsulated, which makes it more robust, easier to maintain and change, and more reusable. For example, where the code needs a stack, that stack is easily borrowed from existing code. In an ordinary procedural language, such a data structure is frequently "wired into" the algorithm and cannot be exported. All of these benefits are especially important for large coding projects that require coordination among many programmers. Here the ability to specify general interfaces for different classes allows each programmer to work on individual code segments with a high degree of integrity.

8.9 Platonism: Object-Oriented Design

C++ gives the programmer the means to implement an OOP design. But how do you develop such a design? No simple methodology exists because each design must be strongly tied to the problem domain and reflect its abstractions. We call this design philosophy Platonism.

In the Platonic paradigm, there is an ideal object. For example, we imagine an ideal chair and attempt to describe its characteristics. These would be characteristics shared by all chairs. Such a chair would be a subclass of ideal furniture. In turn, it may give rise to subcategories, such as swivel chairs, reclining chairs, and beach chairs. Useful descriptions would require expertise on chairs and agreement among the community of chair users. The Platonic chair should be easily modified to describe most commonly occurring chairs. The Platonic chair should be described in terms consistent with existing chair terminology.

C++ was influenced by Simula 67, a language specifically invented for simulations. The Platonic paradigm is a modeling or simulation of the concrete world. It requires that an extra effort be made in determining a design. The design typically provides a public interface that is convenient, general, and efficient. These considerations can be in conflict. Again, there are no simple rules for deciding among such tradeoffs.

The extra effort made should lead to results that offset the increased initial design cost. First and foremost, such effort imposes an additional level of discipline on the programming process. Increasing programmer discipline always pay dividends. Second, it encapsulates into classes related pieces of code. Encapsulation and decomposition always pay dividends. Third, it enhances code reuse through inheritance and ADTs. Code reuse always pays dividends. Fourth, it improves prototyping by deferring implementation decisions and providing access to large, easily used general libraries. Cheap prototyping always pays dividends.

The Platonic paradigm using OOP techniques is quietly revolutionizing the programming process. It does not displace older techniques, such as structured programming, but instead uses them in the small to effectively manage the composition of large and more robust software.

8.10 Turbo C++ Considerations

Multiple inheritance is a complex feature of the language. To get some feeling for its actual use in a detailed example, it is worth while to browse through the *iostream.h* file. The class `iostream` inherits from both `istream` and `ostream`. These share a common base class `ios`. These classes reuse code as a consequence of multiple inheritance.

Inheritance creates the possibility of simpler programs because of code reuse and dynamic typing. Code reuse is maximized by using `protected` access in place of `private` access. These two access categories are equivalent for ordinary client use of their public member functions. Virtual functions allow dynamic typing to be used in selecting member function invocation for publically derived classes.

Turbo C++ implements abstract classes and pure virtual functions. Abstract base classes cannot be used to declare variables. Earlier C++ compilers did not have such classes and simulated them with ordinary virtual functions. This technique was error prone. If the programmer forgets to write out the derived class version of the base class virtual function, the program would invoke the base class function. Turbo C++ will catch this error at compile time.

We can see this behavior by changing the code from Section 8.2 as follows:

```
class data {
        //simulate abstract class - root of type hierarchy
public:
    virtual void print() { } //dummy
};

class person : public virtual data {
protected:
    char        f_name[10], l_name[20];
    int         age;
    long int    soc_sec;
public:
    person();
    person(const char* fn, const char* ln, int a, long int ss);
};
```

Errors will occur at run-time. But if the abstract class is used, the omission of print() in the derived class gives the syntax error message:

```
Pure function 'data::print()' not overridden in 'person'
```

Summary

1. Multiple inheritance allows a derived class to inherit from more than one base class. The syntax of class headers is extended to allow a list, after the colon, of base classes and their privacy designation.

2. The early releases of C++ left unspecified the order of execution for initializing constructors in base and member constructors. With the addition of multiple inheritance, however, it became unnecessarily hazardous to continue this laxness. The current ordering is:

   a. Explicit reference to base class constructors in the order in which they are listed after the header colon.

   b. Unmentioned base classes in the order in which they are declared.

   c. Explicit reference to member class constructors in the order in which they are listed after the header colon.

3. For early C++ compilers, user types had, by default, bitwise assignment. Current systems default to a more sophisticated member-by-member assignment. This rule is recursive until components that are built-in types

are assigned in the usual way. The same idea applies to default initialization.

4. A further change allows the operators `new` and `delete` to be overloaded. This feature provides a simple mechanism for user-defined manipulation of free store. Other technical changes include the ability to overload the operator `->`, distinguishing between signed and unsigned by the overloading selection algorithm, and the use of the scope resolution operator to define pointer to member types.

5. Large C programs are partitioned into multifile units that can be compiled separately. Linking such separate modules requires resolving external references. In C++, these rules are explicit. The key rule is that external nonstatic variables must be defined in exactly one place. Static external constructs are local to a given file. Use of the keyword `extern` together with an initializer constitutes defining a variable. Using the keyword `extern` without an initializer constitutes a declaration but not a definition.

6. An iterator is a mechanism for accessing all components of a given type. The `for` statement provides a built-in iterator for simple arrays. Classes allow data to be hidden from general access, and, typically, an iterator needs to be either a member function or a friend function of the class.

7. C++ supports object-oriented programming (OOP). The central feature of this method is its encapsulation of an appropriate set of data types and their operations (ADTs). The class, with its member functions and operator overloading, provides an appropriate coding tool. A further key idea in OOP is its promotion of code reuse through the inheritance mechanism. The `virtual` function also provides the ability to bind type at run-time. Classes also provide data hiding. Access privileges can be managed and limited to whatever group of functions truly needs access to implementation details.

8. C++ was influenced by Simula 67, a language specifically invented for simulations. The Platonic paradigm is a modeling or simulation of the concrete world. It requires that an extra step be made to define a hierarchy of types in determining a design. The design typically provides a public interface that is convenient, general, and efficient.

Exercises

1. What happens if you attempt to compile:

    ```
    struct A : B {
       int i;
    };

    struct B : A {
       int j;
    };
    ```

2. From Section 8.1, use the class plans and the function foo to see how your compiler detects the inherent ambiguous reference to cost. Change the example to avoid this problem.

3. Among the useful standard headers is *assert.h*. It provides an assertion mechanism:

    ```
    assert(expression);
    ```

    If the *expression* evaluates to *false*, the program terminates with an error indication that includes the file name and source line of the failure.

    We want to write a portable factorial program. As written, the following program overflows on most machines:

    ```
    #include <iostream.h>
    #include <limits.h>
    #include <assert.h>

    long fact(int n)
    {
       if (n <= 1)
          return (1);
       else
          return (fact(n - 1) * n);
    }

    main()
    {
       for (int i = 0; i < 25; ++i)
          cout << i << "   fact    " << fact(i) << "\n";
    }
    ```

    Add assertions to protect against system-dependent integer overflow.

4. The *assert.h* has the lines:

    ```
    #ifdef NDEBUG
    #define assert(EX)
        . . .
    ```

    Explain how this allows a compiler flag to turn off the assertion mechanism.

5. In the program *ptr_mem*, replace the line

    ```
    a.*pXint += 1;
    ```

    by the line

    ```
    ++a.*pXint;
    ```

    This worked under AT&T Release 1.2. Why doesn't it work under Turbo C++? It can be corrected with parentheses. Explain.

6. From Section 8.6, we change the second `for` statement in `main` to the following:

    ```
    for (i = 0; i < w.size(); i += 2)
        cout << (w_it.next() = 2 * i) << "\t";
    ```

    Explain what gets printed.

7. What if the `for` loop in the previous exercise were changed to the following:

    ```
    for (i = 0; i < w.size(); ++i) {
        w_it.next() = 2 * i;
        cout << w_it.next() << "\t";
    }
    cout << w;
    ```

    Explain what gets printed.

8. Define the classes

    ```
    class business : public virtual data {
    protected:
        char      b_name[20];
        char      b_addr[80];
        long int phone;
    public:
        business();
    ```

```
        business(const char* bn, const char* ba, long int pn);
        void print();
};

class bus_pers : public person, public business {
    . . .
};
```

Now write all the member functions and a `main()` to test the material in Section 8.2. Discuss the design aspects of using multiple inheritance to collect the joint information across several classes. A possible design could be a class whose members are variables of each of these types. Another design could be a class derived from the previous class adding information members. An appropriate design might depend on what is already available and reusable.

9. Use the Turbo C++ *graphics.h* to program a box-drawing and a triangle-drawing program. Have each of these class be derived from an abstract class `shape`.

10. Develop a message class to work in graphics mode. Have a class `location` as a base class for drawing both shapes and messages. Now use the design from Exercise 8.9 to develop both triangles and boxes that contain messages. You may want to use multiple inheritance for this exercise. Also see Borland's *Turbo C++ Getting Started Manual*, pp. 151–156, or you may have on line their code for *mcircle.cpp*.

Appendix A

ASCII Character Codes

Left/Right Digits	ASCII									
	American Standard Code for Information Interchange									
	0	1	2	3	4	5	6	7	8	9
0	nul	soh	stx	etx	eot	enq	ack	bel	bs	ht
1	nl	vt	np	cr	so	si	dle	dc1	dc2	dc3
2	dc4	nak	syn	etb	can	em	sub	esc	fs	gs
3	rs	us	sp	!	"	#	$	%	&	'
4	(	)	*	+	,	–	.	/	0	1
5	2	3	4	5	6	7	8	9	:	;
6	<	=	>	?	@	A	B	C	D	E
7	F	G	H	I	J	K	L	M	N	O
8	P	Q	R	S	T	U	V	W	X	Y
9	Z	[	\	]		_	`	a	b	c
10	d	e	f	g	h	i	j	k	l	m
11	n	o	p	q	r	s	t	u	v	w
12	x	y	z	{	|	}	~	del		

Some Observations

1. Character codes 0–31 and 127 are nonprinting.

2. Character code 32 prints a single space.

3. Character codes for digits 0 through 9 are contiguous.

229

4. Character codes for letters A through Z are contiguous.

5. Character codes for letters a through z are contiguous.

6. The difference between a capital letter and the corresponding lowercase letter is 32.

The Meaning of Some of the Abbreviations					
nul	null	bel	bell	bs	backspace
ht	horizontal tab	nl	newline	vt	vertical tab
cr	carriage return	esc	escape		

Appendix B

Operator Precedence and Associativity

The following is the precedence and associativity table for all the C++ operators. In case of doubt, parenthesize.

Operators	Associativity
: :	left to right
() [] -> . *postfix*++ *postfix*--	left to right
++ -- ! ~ sizeof (*type*) + (unary) – (unary) * (indirection) & (address) new delete	right to left
.* ->*	left to right
* / %	left to right
+ –	left to right
<< >>	left to right
< <= > >=	left to right
== !=	left to right
&	left to right
	left to right
		left to right
&&	left to right
||	left to right
?:	right to left
= += -= *= /= *etc*	right to left
(comma operator)	left to right

Appendix C

Turbo C++ Language Guide

This appendix is a concise guide to C++. It summarizes many of the key language elements of C++ that are not found in older procedural languages, such as Pascal and C. It is intended as a convenient guide to the language for C programmers who have read this text.

232

C.1 Keywords

Keywords are explicitly reserved identifiers that have a strict meaning in C++. They cannot be redefined or used in other contexts.

Keywords

asm	continue	float	new	signed	try
auto	default	for	operator	sizeof	typedef
break	delete	friend	private	static	union
case	do	goto	protected	struct	unsigned
catch	double	if	public	switch	virtual
char	else	inline	register	template	void
class	enum	int	return	this	volatile
const	extern	long	short	throw	while

C++ implementations can have the additional keyword

```
overload
```

This is considered an anachronism in Turbo C++.

The keywords

```
catch        template        throw        try
```

are experimental and are reserved for implementing exception handling and parameterized types. Other keywords that are specific to Turbo C++, such as `near` and `far`, can be found in your Borland manual.

C.2 Constants

Constants are largely as in ANSI C. Differences include: the scope rules for enumerators, the enumerator type in C++ is uniquely its enumeration name but in C it is an `int`; and a character constant in C++ is `char` but in C it is an `int`.

Enumerations (see Section 2.3) define named `int` constants. They can be anonymous, as in

```
enum {false, true};
```

They can be their own type, as in

```
enum color {red, blue, white, green, orange};
```

The keyword `const` (see Section 2.2) is used to declare that an object's value is constant throughout its scope.

```
const int N = 100;
double w[N];      //N may be used in a constant expression

const  int bus_stops[5] = {23, 44, 57, 59, 83};
//The element values, bus_stops[i], are constant.
```

The use of `const` differs from the use of constant definitions by `#define`, as in

```
#define N   100
```

In the `const` case, N is a non-modifiable *lvalue*. In the `define` case, N is a literal.

C.3 Comments

C++ has a one-line comment symbol `//` (see Section 2.1).

```
//Compile with version 1.2 or later
const float pi = 3.14159;  //pi accurate to six places
```

C-style comments are also available.

```
/*   *  *  *  *  *  *
     TURBO C++
     Demonstrate Multiple-Inheritance
     OOP - Platonic Designs
 *   *  *  *  *  *  *  */
```

Comments do not nest.

C.4 Scope Rules

C++ has file scope, function scope, block scope, class scope, and function prototype scope. File scope extends from the point of declaration in a file to the end of that file. Function prototype scope is the scope of identifiers in the function prototype argument list and extends to the end of the declaration. Blocks nest in a conventional way, but functions cannot be declared inside other functions or blocks.

Declarations can occur anywhere in a block (see Sections 1.2, 2.3). A declaration can also be an initializing statement of an outermost `for` statement.

```
for (int i = 0; i < N; ++i) {
    . . .
```

Declarations cannot occur as initializing statements within nested loops. Selection statements such as the `if` or `switch` statement cannot merely control a declaration. In general, jumps and selections cannot bypass an initialization. This is not true of ANSI C.

```
if (flag)
    int j = 6;       //illegal
else
    int j = 19;

if (flag) {
    int j = 6;          //legal within block
    cout << j ;
}
```

Class member identifiers are local to that class. The scope resolution operator : : can be used to resolve ambiguities (see Section 2.5).

```
class A {
public:
    int  i;
    void foo();
};

class B {
public:
    char i;
    void foo() {  A :: foo(); . . .}
};
```

A hidden external name can be accessed by using the scope resolution operator.

```
int   i;
void   foo(int   i)
{
    i = ::i;
    . . .
}
```

A hidden `class`, `struct`, `union`, or `enum` identifier can be accessed by using its respective keyword.

```
static union u {
    . . .
};

void foo(int u)
{
    union u U;
    . . .
}
```

Classes can be nested. The rules for nesting classes are in transition. C++ Release 2.0 rules state that the inner class is not inside the scope of the outer class but rather has the same scope as the outer class. Since this can lead to confusion, nesting class declarations is normally poor style. New rules are being proposed that will make the inner class scoped within the outer class. The safest current policy is to avoid this construction.

Enumerations declared inside a class, as in

```
class foo_bool {
public:
    enum boolean {false, true} flag;
};

main()
{
    boolean  b = foo_bool::true;   //legal under 2.0 rules
    foo_bool c;
    c.flag = false;   //illegal need foo_bool::false
    . . .
}
```

make the enumerators have class scope, but `boolean` is a global type as currently defined by Release 2.0. This is expected to change when new rules for nesting are implemented. For the moment it is best to avoid these nested declarations.

C.5 Linkage Rules

Modern systems are built around multifile inclusion, compilation, and linkage. For C and C++, it is necessary to understand how multifile programs are combined. Linking separate modules requires resolving external references. The key rule is that external nonstatic variables must be defined in exactly one place. Use of the keyword `extern` together with an initializer constitutes defining a variable. Using the keyword `extern` without an initializer constitutes a declaration but not a definition. The following example illustrates these rules:

```
//file prog1.c
   char   c;            //definition of c
   . . .

//file prog2.c
   extern char c;       //declaration of c
   . . .

//file prog3.c
   extern int n = 5;    //definition of n
   . . .

//file prog4.c
   char         c;      //illegal second definition
   extern float n;      //illegal type mismatch
   extern int   k;      //illegal no declaration
   . . .
```

Constant definitions and `inline` definitions at file scope are local to that file unless explicitly declared `extern`. It is usual to place such definitions in a header file to be included with any code that needs these definitions.

A `typedef` declaration is local to its file. It is a synonym for the type it defines.

```
typedef char *c_string;    //c_string is pointer to char
typedef void (*ptr_f)();   //pointer to function
                           //of no arguments returning void
```

Enumerators are local to their file. Enumerators and typedefs that are needed in a multifile program should be placed in a header file. Enumerators defined within a class are local to that class. Access to them requires the scope resolution operator.

```
//types.h    header file
typedef char *c_string;    //c_string is pointer to char
typedef void (*ptr_f)();   //pointer to function

void foo(c_string s);      //function prototypes
void title();
void pr_onoff();

enum {OFF, ON};
extern int x;

//fcns.c to be separately compiled
#include <iostream.h>
#include "types.h"

typedef char *c_string;    //c_string is pointer to char
typedef void (*ptr_f)();   //pointer to function

void foo(c_string s)
{
   cout <<"\noutput: " << s;
}

void title()
{
   cout << "\nTEST TYPEDEFS";
}

void pr_onoff()
{
   if (x == OFF)
       cout << "\nOFF";
   else
       cout << "\nON";
}
```

```
//linkage_ex.c    main program file   CC fcns.o linkage_ex.c
#include <iostream.h>
#include "types.h"
int x = 0;

main()
{
    c_string f = "foo on you";
    ptr_f    pf = &pr_onoff;

    foo("ENTER 0 or 1: ");
    if (( cin >> x) == ON)
        pf = &title;
    pr_onoff();
    pf();
    x = !x;
    pf();
    foo(f);
}
```

C.6 Types

The fundamental types in C++ are the same as in C, with the following ANSI C extensions (see Sections 2.3, 2.4, 2.6). Both `signed` and `void` types are available.

The derived types have significant extensions, including generic pointer type `void*` . Both anonymous unions and anonymous enumerations are allowed, and there is also a reference type. An anonymous union can only have public data members. A file scope anonymous union has to be declared `static`. The `class` type (see Chapter 3) is another extension, and the `struct` is extended to be a variant of the `class`. Union, enumeration, and class names are type names.

```
void*   gen_ptr;              //a generic pointer
int     i, &ref_i = i;        //ref_i is an alias for i
enum    boolean {false, true}; //enumeration
boolean flag;                 //boolean is now a type name
```

```
class    card {                      //user-defined type
   int   cd;                         //private data member
public:
   suit s;                           //public data member
   pips p;
   void pr_card();                   //member function
};
suit card::* ptr_s = &card::s;   //pointer to member
```

C.7 Conversion Rules

C and C++ have numerous conversion rules. Many of these conversions are implicit, which makes C convenient but potentially dangerous for the novice. Implicit conversions can induce run-time bugs that are hard to detect.

The standard C conversions apply in C++. Implicit pointer conversions also occur in C++ (see Section 5.1). Any pointer type can be converted to a generic pointer of type void* . However, unlike ANSI C, a generic pointer is not assignment compatible with an arbitrary pointer type. This means that C++ requires that generic pointers be cast to an explicit type for assignment to a non-generic pointer variable.

```
char* mem;
void* gen_p;
gen_p = mem;             //C and C++
mem   = (char*)gen_p;    //C and C++
mem   = gen_p;           //legal C and illegal C++
```

The name of an array is a pointer to its base element. The null pointer value can be converted to any type. A pointer to a class can be converted to a pointer to a publicly derived base class (see Section 6.4). This also applies to references. C++ is generally stricter than traditional C and does not allow mixing of pointer types unless they are correctly cast. As in ANSI C, float expressions need not be automatically converted to double.

Traditional C casts are augmented in C++ by a functional notation as a syntactic alternative (see Section 5.2). A functional notation of the form

type-name (*expression*)

is equivalent to a cast. The type must be expressible as an identifier. Thus the two expressions

```
x = float(i);   //C++ functional notation
x = (float) i;  //C  cast notation
```

are equivalent. Functional notation is the preferred style.

A constructor of one argument is de facto a type conversion from the argument's type to the constructor's class type. Consider an example of a `string` constructor (see Section 4.3):

```
string::string(const char* p)
{
    len = strlen(p);
    s = new char[len + 1];
    strcpy(s, p);
}
```

This is automatically a type transfer from `char*` to `string`. These conversions are from an already defined type to a user-defined type. However, it is not possible for the user to add a constructor to a built-in type—for example, to `int` or `double`. In the `string` example, one may also want a conversion from `string` to `char*`. This can be done by defining a special conversion function inside the `string` class as follows:

```
operator (char *)() { return s; }   //recall char *s; is a member
```

The general form of such a member function is

```
operator type() { ... }
```

These conversions occur implicitly in assignment expressions and in argument and return conversions from functions.

Temporaries can be created by the compiler to facilitate these operations. This can require constructor invocation. This is system- and compiler-dependent. It may dramatically and unexpectedly affect execution speeds.

C.8 Expressions and Operators

C++ is an operator-rich language that is expression oriented. The operators have seventeen precedence levels. Operators also can have side effects. Appendix B lists their precedence and associativity.

C++ has additional novel operators not found in C. C++ introduces the operator : :, called the scope resolution operator. When used in the form : : *variable*, it allows access to the externally named variable (see Section 2.5). Other uses of this notation are important for classes.

The unary operators `new` and `delete` are available to manipulate *free store* (see Section 2.10). Free store is a system-provided memory pool for objects whose lifetime is directly managed by the programmer. The programmer creates the object by using `new` and destroys the object by using `delete`.

The operator `new` is used in the following forms:

```
new type-name
new type-name initializer
new (type-name)
```

In each case there are at least two effects. First, an appropriate amount of store is allocated from free store to contain the named type. Second, the base address of the object is returned as the value of the `new` expression. If `new` fails, the null pointer value `0` is returned. The expression is of type `void*` and can be assigned to any pointer type variable. An initializer is a parenthesized list of arguments. For a simple type, such as an `int`, it would be a single expression. It cannot be used to initialize arrays, but it can be an argument list to an appropriate constructor.

The operator `delete` destroys an object created by `new`, in effect returning its allocated storage to free store for reuse. The following example uses these constructs to dynamically allocate an array:

```
//Use of new operator to dynamically allocate an array.

#include <iostream.h>

main()
{
    int* data;
    int  size;

    cout << "\nEnter array size: ";
    cin >> size;

    data = new int[size];
    for (int j = 0; j < size; ++j)
        cout << (data[j] = j) << "\t";
    cout << "\n\n";
    delete data;
    . . .

}
```

The pointer variable `data` is used as the base address of a dynamically allocated array whose number of elements is the value of `size`. The `new` operator is used to allocate from free store sufficient storage for an object of type `int[size]`. The operator `delete` returns to free store the storage associated with the pointer variable `data`. This can be done only with objects allocated by `new`. There are no guarantees on what values will appear in objects allocated from free store. The programmer is responsible for properly initializing such objects.

The operator `delete` is used in the following forms:

> `delete` *expression*
> `delete` [*expression*] *expression*

The first form is the most common. The expression is typically a pointer variable used in a previous `new` expression. The second form is occasionally used when returning store that was allocated as an array type. The bracketed expression gives the number of elements of the array. The operator `delete` returns a value of type `void`.

C.9 Classes

C++ and C have structures; they are forms of heterogeneous aggregate types. C++ redefines structures to allow data hiding, inheritance, and member functions as major new extensions. In C++, the new keyword `class` (Chapter 3) or the keyword `struct` are used to declare user-defined types. An example is:

```
class vect {
private:
    int* p;                             //base pointer
    int size;                           //number of elements
public:
    //constructors and destructor
    vect() { size = 10; p = new int[10]} //create a size 10 array
    vect(int n);                        //create a size n array
    vect(vect& v);                      //initialization by vect
    vect(int a[], int n);               //initialization by array
    ~vect() { delete p; }               //destructor
    //other member functions
    int  ub() { return (size - 1); }    //upper bound
    int& operator [](int i);            //obtain range checked element
};
```

The keywords `public`, `private`, and `protected` indicate the visibility of members that follow (see Sections 3.5 and 6.2). The default for `class` is `private`, and for `struct` is `public`. In the above example, the data members p and `size` are `private`. This makes them visible solely to member functions of the same class.

C.9.1 Constructors and Destructors

A constructor is a member function whose name is the same as the class name (see Section 4.1). It *constructs* objects of the class type. This involves initialization of data members and frequently free store allocation using `new`. For classes with constructors, if they have a constructor with a void argument list, then they can be a base type of an array declaration, where initialization is not explicit. The constructor of no arguments is called the *default constructor*.

```
foo::foo() { . . .}   //default constructor
//The following is a default constructor on some compilers
hoo::hoo(int i = 0) { . . .}
```

A destructor is a member function whose name is the class name preceded by the character ~ (tilde) (see Section 4.2). Its usual purpose is to *destroy* values of the class type. This is typically accomplished by using `delete`.

A constructor of the form

```
type::type(type& x)
```

is used to perform copying of one *type* value into another when:

1. A *type* variable is initialized by a *type* value.

2. A *type* value is passed as an argument in a function.

3. A *type* value is returned from a function.

In older C++ systems, if this constructor was not present, then these operations were bitwise copy. In newer systems, the default is member-by-member assignment of value.

Classes with constructors having an empty argument list can have a derived array type. For example,

```
vect a[5];
```

is a declaration that uses the empty argument constructor to create an array a of five objects, each of which is a size 10 `vect`.

A class having members whose type requires a constructor may have these specified after the argument list for its own constructor (see Section 4.5). The constructor has a comma-separated list of constructor calls following a colon. The constructor is invoked by using the member name followed by a parenthesized argument list. Constructors cannot be virtual, but destructors can be virtual. Constructors and destructors are not inherited.

C.9.2 Member Functions

Member functions are functions declared within a class and, as a consequence, have access to `private`, `protected`, and `public` members of that class (see Section 3.4). If defined inside the class, they are treated as `inline` functions and are also treated when necessary as overloaded functions. In the class `vect`, the member function

```
int  ub() { return (size - 1); }   //upper bound
```

is defined. In this example, the member function ub is inline and has access to the private member size.

Member functions are invoked normally by use of the "." or -> operators, as in

```
vect  a(20), b;                //invoke appropriate constructor
vect* ptr_v = &b;
int   uba = a.ub(), ubb;        //invoke member ub
ubb = ptr_v -> ub();            //invoke member ub
```

C.9.3 The this Pointer

The keyword this denotes an implicitly declared self-referential pointer (see Section 4.8). It can be used in a non-static member function. A simple illustration of its use is as follows:

```
// Use of the this pointer

class c_pair {
   char     c1, c2;
public:
   c_pair(char b) { c1 = 1 + (c2 = b); }
   c_pair increment() { c1++; c2++; return (*this); }
   unsigned where_am_I() { return ((unsigned)this); }
   void print() { cout << c1 << c2 << "\t"; }
};
```

The member function increment() uses the implicitly provided pointer this to return the newly incremented value of both c1 and c2. The member function where_am_I() returns the address of the given object. The this keyword provides for a built-in self-referential pointer. It's as if c_pair implicitly declared the private member c_pair* const this.

Early C++ systems allowed memory management for objects to be controlled by assignment to the this pointer. Such code is obsolete because the this pointer is nonmodifiable.

C.9.4 static and const Member Functions

An ordinary member function invoked as

```
object.mem(i, j, k);
```

has an explicit argument list i, j, k and an implicit argument list that are the members of *object*. The implicit arguments can be thought of as a list of arguments accessible through the this pointer. In contrast, a static member function cannot access any of the members using the this pointer. A const member function cannot modify its implicit arguments. The following example illustrates these differences:

```
//Salary calculation using
//static and constant member functions.

#include <iostream.h>

class salary {
    int         b_sal;
    int         your_bonus;
    static int all_bonus;   //declaration
public:
    salary(int b) : b_sal(b) { }
    void calc_bonus(double perc) { your_bonus = b_sal * perc; }
    static void reset_all(int p) { all_bonus = p; }
    int comp_tot() const
        { return (b_sal + your_bonus + all_bonus); }
};

int salary::all_bonus = 100; //declaration and definition

main()
{
    salary w1(1000), w2(2000);

    w1.calc_bonus(0.2);
    w2.calc_bonus(0.15);
    salary::reset_all(400);
    cout << " w1 " << w1.comp_tot() << "    w2 " << w2.comp_tot()
        << "\n";
}
```

The static member all_bonus requires a file scope declaration. It exists independently of any specific variables of type salary being declared. The static member can also be referred to as:

```
salary::all_bonus
```

The const modifier comes between the end of the argument list and the front of the code body. It indicates that no data members will have their values changed. As such it makes the code more robust. In effect it means that the self-referential pointer is passed as `const salary* const this`.

A `static` member function can be invoked using the scope resolution operator.

C.9.5 Inheritance

Inheritance is the mechanism of *deriving* a new class from an old one (Chapter 6). The existing class can be added to or altered to create the derived class. A class can be derived from an existing class using the form:

```
class class-name :  (public|private) optional base-class-name
{
    member  declarations
};
```

As usual, the keyword `class` can be replaced by the keyword `struct`, with the usual implication that members are default `public`. The keywords `public`, `private`, and `protected` are available as visibility modifiers for class members (see Section 6.2). A `public` member is visible throughout its scope. A `private` member is visible to other member functions within its own class. A `protected` member is visible to other member functions within its class and any class immediately derived from it. These visibility modifiers can be used within a class declaration in any order and with any frequency.

A base class having a constructor with arguments requires that a class derived from it have a constructor. The form of such a constructor is:

```
class-name(argument list) : base-class-name :(base class argument list)
{
    . . .
};
```

The base class argument list is used when invoking the appropriate base class constructor and is executed before the body of the derived class constructor is executed.

A publicly derived class is a *subtype* of its base class (see Section 6.4). A variable of the derived class can in many ways be treated as if it were the base class type. A pointer whose type is pointer to base class can point to objects having the publicly derived class type. A reference to the derived class, when meaningful, may be implicitly converted to a reference to the public base class. It is possible to declare a reference to a base class and initialize it to an object of the publicly derived class.

The following is an example of a derived class:

```
class vect_bnd : public vect {
    int l_bnd, u_bnd;
public:
    vect_bnd();
    vect_bnd(int, int);
    int& operator[](int);
    int   ub() { return (u_bnd); }
    int   lb() { return (l_bnd); }
};

vect_bnd::vect_bnd() : vect(10)
{
    l_bnd = 0;
    u_bnd = 9;
}

vect_bnd::vect_bnd(int lb, int ub) : vect(ub - lb + 1)
{
    l_bnd = lb;
    u_bnd = ub;
}
```

In this example, the constructors for the derived class invoke a constructor in the base class with argument list following the colon.

C.9.6 Multiple Inheritance

Multiple inheritance allows a derived class to be derived from more than one base class (Chapter 8). The syntax of class headers is extended to allow a list of base classes and their privacy designation. An example is:

```
class tools {
    . . .
};
```

```
class parts {
    . . .

};

class labor {
    . . .

};

class plans : public tools, public parts, public labor {
    . . .

};
```

In this example, the derived class `plans` publicly inherits the members of all three base classes. This parental relationship is described by the inheritance *directed acyclic graph* (DAG). The DAG is a graph structure whose nodes are classes and whose directed edges point from base to derived class.

In deriving an identically named member from different classes, ambiguities may arise. These derivations are allowed provided the user does not make an ambiguous reference to such a member.

With multiple inheritance, two base classes can be derived from a common ancestor. If both base classes are used in the ordinary way by their derived class, that class will have two subobjects of the common ancestor. This duplication, if not desirable, can be eliminated by using `virtual` inheritance (see Section 8.1).

C.9.7 Constructor Invocation

The early releases of C++ left unspecified the order of execution for initializing constructors in base and member constructors. Most of the time these constructions were independent of each other, and the results were independent of order. With the addition of multiple inheritance, however, it became unnecessarily hazardous to continue this laxness. Thus the current ordering is:

1. Explicit reference to base class constructors in the order in which they are listed after the header colon.

2. Unmentioned base classes in the order in which they are declared.

3. Explicit reference to member class constructors in the order in which they are listed after the header colon.

Virtual base classes have special precedence and are constructed before any of their derived classes. They are constructed before any nonvirtual base classes. Their construction order depends on their DAG. It is a depth-first, left-to-right order. Destructors are invoked in reverse order of constructors. These rules, although complicated, should conform to one's intuition, and a client program's correctness should not depend on constructor/destructor ordering. Finally, the associated destructors are called in the reverse order from constructor invocation.

Let us illustrate by elaborating on a previous example.

```
class tools {
   . . .
public:
   tools(char*);
   ~tools();
   . . .
};

class parts {
   . . .
public:
   parts(char*);
   ~parts();
   . . .
};

class labor {
   . . .
public:
   labor(int);
   ~labor();
   . . .
};

class plans : public tools, public parts, public labor {
   . . .
   special a;   //member class with constructor
public:
   plans(int m) : labor(m), tools("lathe"), a(m), parts("widget")
       { . . . }
   ~plans();
   . . .
};
```

In this case, the member constructor a(m) appears before the base class constructor parts("widget") but by our rules is invoked last. Since its constructor was last, its destructor is invoked first, followed by ~parts, ~tools, ~labor, and ~plans.

C.9.8 Abstract Base Classes

A pure virtual function is a virtual member function whose body is undefined (see Section 8.2). Notationally, it is declared inside the class as follows:

```
virtual function prototype = 0;
```

A derived class must define or declare each pure virtual function in its immediate base class. A class that has at least one *pure virtual* function is an *abstract class*.

C.9.9 Pointer to Class Member

C uses pointers to structures and a simple accessing scheme to pick off a member value. In C++, pointer to class member is *distinct* from a pointer to class. A pointer to class member has type $T::*$, where T is the class name. C++ has two operators that act to dereference a pointer to class member. The pointer to member operators are:

```
.*    and   ->*
```

Think of *obj.*ptr_mem* as first dereferencing the pointer to obtain a member variable and then accessing the member for the designated *obj* (see Section 8.4).

C.10 Functions

In C, functions are strictly call-by-value. Changes in C++ to how functions work include use of function prototypes, overloading, call-by-reference, default arguments, and the effects of the keywords inline, friend, and virtual.

C.10.1 Prototypes

In C++, the prototype form is (see Section 2.6):

> *type name* (*argument-declaration-list*) ;

Examples are:

```
double sqrt(double x);
void   pr_int(char*, int);      //definition contains names
void   print(const char* s);    //s is not changed
int    printf(char* format, ...); //variable number of args.
```

With the above `sqrt` prototype definition, invoking `sqrt` guarantees that, if feasible, an argument will be converted to type `double`. Prototypes are also found in ANSI C and greatly improve type checking.

C.10.2 Overloading

The term *overloading* refers to use of the same name for multiple meanings of an operator or a function (see Section 2.9). The meaning selected will depend on the types of the arguments used by the operator or function (see Section 5.3).

Consider a function that averages the values in an array of `double` versus one that averages the values in an array of `int`. Both are conveniently named `avg_arr`.

```
double   avg_arr(const double a[], int size);
double   avg_arr(const int a[], int size);

double avg_arr(const int a[], int size)
{
    int  sum = 0;

    for (int i = 0; i < size; ++i)
        sum += a[i];                 //performs int arithmetic
    return ((double) sum / size);
}
```

```
double avg_arr(const double a[], int size)
{
   double  sum = 0.0;

   for (int i = 0; i < size; ++i)
      sum += a[i];                   //performs double arithmetic
   return (sum / size);
}
```

In early systems, the keyword overload was used to declare a non-member function name as overloadable. This practice is allowed but obsolete.

The function argument type list is called its *signature*. The return type is not a part of the signature, but the order of the arguments is crucial.

```
int  sqr(int i);            //signature is int
double  sqr(int i);         //signature is int
void print(int i = 0);      //signature is int
void print(int i, double x); //signature is int, double
void print(double y, int i); //signature is double, int
```

In this example sqr() is illegally redeclared, but print() has three distinct signatures. When the print() function is invoked, the Turbo C++ compiler matches the actual arguments to the different signatures and picks the best match. In general, there are three possibilities: a best match, an ambiguous match, and no match. Without a best match, the compiler issues an appropriate syntax error.

```
print('A');                 //converts and matches int
print(str[]);               //no match wrong type
print(15, 9);               //ambiguous
print(15, 9.0);             //matches int, double
print();                    //match  int by default
```

There are two parts to the signature matching algorithm. The first part determines a best match for each argument. The second part sees if there is one function that is a uniquely best match in each argument.

For a given argument, a best match is always an exact match. An exact match also includes *trivial conversions*. For type T these are:

From	To
//equally good	
T	T
T	T&
T&	T
T	const T
T	volatile T
T[]	T*
//not as good	
T*	const T*
T*	volatile T*
T&	const T&
T&	volatile T&

The first six trivial conversions cannot be used to disambiguate exact matches. The last four are considered worse than the first six. Thus

```
void print( int i);
void print( const int& i);
```

can be unambiguously overloaded.

The simplified rule in Section 5.3 is replaced by a two-part rule that distinguishes promotions from other standard conversions. A promotion is going from a narrower type to a wider type. Thus going from char to int is a promotion. Promotions are better than other standard conversions. Among promotions, conversion from float to double and conversion using only integral promotion are better than other promotions. Standard conversions also include pointer conversions.

Whichever overloaded function is to be invoked, the invocation argument list must be matched to the declaration parameter list. The matching algorithm is as follows:

Overloaded Function Selection Algorithm

1. Use an exact match if found.

2. Try standard type promotions.

3. Try standard type conversions.

4. Try user-defined conversions.

5. Use a match to ellipsis if found.

An exact match is clearly best. Casts can be used to force such a match. The compiler will complain about ambiguous situations. Thus, it is poor practice to rely on subtle type distinctions and implicit conversions that obscure the overloaded function that is called. When in doubt use explicit conversions to provide an exact match.

C.10.3 Call-by-Reference

Reference declarations allow C++ to have *call-by-reference* arguments (see Section 2.7). Let us use this mechanism to write a function `greater` that exchanges two values if the first is greater than the second.

```
int greater(int& a, int& b)
{
    if (a > b) {       //exchange
        int temp = a;
        a = b;
        b = temp;
        return (1);
    }
    else
        return (0);
}
```

Now, if `i` and `j` are two `int` variables, then

```
greater(i, j)
```

will use the reference to `i` and the reference to `j` to exchange, if necessary, their two values. In traditional C, this must be accomplished using pointers and indirection.

```
/* traditional C greater  */
int greater(int* a, int* b)
{
    if (*a > *b) {    //exchange
        int temp = *a;
        *a = *b;
        *b = temp;
        return (1);
    }
    else
        return (0);
}
```

C.10.4 Inline

The keyword `inline` suggests to the compiler that the function be converted to inline code (see Section 2.2). This keyword is used for the sake of efficiency, and generally with short functions, and is implicit for member functions that are defined within their class. A compiler can ignore this directive for a variety of reasons, including the fact that the function is too long. In those cases, the `inline` function is compiled as an ordinary function. An example is:

```
inline float circum(float rad) { return (pi * 2 * rad); }
```

Inline functions are of internal linkage unless explicitly declared `extern`.

C.10.5 Default Arguments

A formal parameter can be given a default argument (see Section 2.8). However, this can be done only with contiguous formal parameters that are rightmost in the parameter list. A default value is usually an appropriate constant that occurs frequently when the function is called. The following function illustrates this point:

```
int mult(int n, int k = 2)     //k = 2 is default
{
    if (k == 2)
        return (n * n);
    else
        return (mult(n, k - 1) * n);
}
```

We assume that most of the time the function is used to return the value of n squared.

C.10.6 Friend Functions

The keyword `friend` is a function specifier (see Section 5.4). It allows a nonmember function access to the hidden members of the class of which it is a friend. Its use is a method of escaping the strict strong typing and data hiding restrictions of C++. A `friend` function must appear inside the class declaration of which it is a friend. It is prefaced by the keyword `friend` and can appear anywhere in the class. Member functions of one class can be `friend` functions of another class. In this case, the member function is written in the friend's class using the scope resolution operator to qualify its function name. If all member functions of one class are friend functions of a second class, this can be specified by writing `friend class` *class name*.

The following declarations are typical:

```
class tweedledee {
   . . .
   friend void alice();        //friend function
   int          cheshire();    //member function
   . . .
};

class tweedledum {
   . . .
   friend int tweedledee::cheshire();
   . . .
};

class tweedledumber {
   . . .
   friend class tweedledee;    //all member functions
                               //of tweedledee have access
   . . .
};
```

C.10.7 Operator Overloading

A special case of function overloading is operator overloading (see Section 5.5). The keyword `operator` is used to overload the built-in C operators. Just as a function name, such as `print`, can be given a variety of meanings that depend on its arguments, so can an operator, such as +, be given additional meanings. This allows infix expressions of both user types and built-in types to be written. The precedence and associativity remain fixed.

Operator overloading typically uses either member functions or friend functions because they both have privileged access. Overloading a unary operator using a member function has an empty argument list because the single operator argument is the implicit argument (see Section 5.6). For binary operators, member function operator overloading has, as the first argument, the implicitly passed class variable and, as a second argument, the lone argument list parameter (see Section 5.7). Friend functions or ordinary functions have both arguments specified in the parameter list.

We shall demonstrate how to overload a unary operator, using ++ as an example. We define the class `clock` that can store time as days, hours, minutes, and seconds.

```
class clock {
    unsigned long int  tot_secs, secs, mins, hours, days;
public:
    clock(unsigned long int i); //constructor and conversion
    void print();                    //formatted printout
    void tick();                     //add one second
    clock operator ++() { this -> tick(); return(*this); }
};
```

This class overloads the autoincrement operator. It is a member function and can be invoked on its implicit single argument. The member function `tick` adds one second to the implicit argument of the overloaded ++ operator.

An overloaded operator must have an argument that is of class type. This must be explicit (casting is allowed) and cannot rely on implicit conversions. In this regard an overloaded operator is subtly different than other forms of overloading.

The ternary conditional operator ?:, the scope resolution operator ::, and the two member operators . and .* cannot be overloaded.

Release 2.1 distinguishes between prefix and postfix autoincrement and autodecrement operators. To stay compatible, use only the prefix version of this operator. In the future, postfix can be distinguished by defining the postfix overloaded function as having a single unused integer argument, as in

```
class T {
public:
    void operator++(int);  //postfix invoked as t.operator++(0);
    void operator--(int);
};
```

There will be no implied semantical relationship between the postfix and prefix forms.

C.10.8 Virtual Functions

The keyword `virtual` is a function specifier that provides a mechanism for dynamically selecting at run-time the appropriate member function from among base and derived class functions (see Section 6.5). It may be used only to modify member function declarations. A `virtual` function must be executable code. When invoked, its semantics are the same as other functions. In a derived class, its name can be overloaded, and the function prototype of the derived function must have matching type. The selection of which function to invoke from among a group of overloaded `virtual` functions is dynamic. The typical case is where a base class has a virtual function and derived classes have their versions of this function. A pointer to a base class type can point at either a base class object or a derived class object. The member function to be invoked is selected at run-time. It corresponds to the object's type, not the pointer's type. In the absence of a derived type member, the base class virtual function is used by default.

Consider the following example:

```
//virtual function selection
#include <iostream.h>

class B {
public:
    int  i;
    virtual void print_i() { cout << i << " inside B\n"; }
};

class D : public B {
public:
    void print_i() { cout << i << " inside D\n"; }
};

main()
{
    B   b;
    B*  pb = &b;
    D   f;

    f.i = 1 + (b.i = 1);
    pb -> print_i();
    pb = &f;
    pb -> print_i();
}
```

The output from this program is:

```
1 inside B
2 inside D
```

In each case, a different version of `print_i` is executed. Selection depends dynamically on the object being pointed at.

C.10.9 Type-Safe Linkage

Linkage rules for non-C++ functions can be specified using a *linkage-specification* (see Section 8.5). Some examples are:

```
extern "C" atoi(const char* nptr);   //C linkage

extern "C" {
#include <stdio.h>
}                       //C linkage for these prototypes
```

This specification is at file scope and is system-dependent as to which languages are supported.

C.11 Input/Output

C and C++ import I/O as library functions. This latter approach is more portable. For it to work well, however, the programming community must agree to a basic standard collection of library functions. In C, this library is described by `stdio.h`. It has been in wide use since the mid-1970s and is available for use in C++ programs.

C++ has been developing its own libraries distinct from C. Output is returned to an object of type `ostream` (see Section 7.1). An operator << is overloaded in this class to perform output conversions from standard types. The standard output `ostream` corresponding to `stdout` is `cout`, and the standard output `ostream` corresponding to `stderr` is `cerr`.

Input is returned to an object of type `istream`, as described in *iostream.h* (see Section 7.4). An operator >> is overloaded in this class to perform input conversions to standard types. The standard input `istream` corresponding to `stdin` is `cin`.

C.11.1 Iostream I/O

The header `iostream.h` contains the stream I/O library. It defines the `iostream` class, which inherits both `istream` and `ostream` properties. Both input and output can be performed on such an object. Included are the following:

1. The standard ostream object `clog` provides buffered output to standard error.

2. The format state manipulators `dec`, `hex`, and `oct` change the default integer representation. The stream member function `precision(int)` can be used to set floating point precision.

3. The manipulators `flush` and `endl` are used to immediately print buffered output. The `endl` manipulator also prints a newline.

4. Istream functions `getline(char Buf[], int Limit, char Delim =` `'\n')`, and `gcount()` are used to extract line-at-a-time input. The argument `Limit` is one less than the maximum line length. The delimiter character is by default a newline (also EOF is tested). The line is stored in the character array argument `Buf[]`. A call to `gcount()` gets the number of characters extracted from the input by the last call to `getline()`.

5. The header file *strstream.h* adds functionality that allows streams to be processed as strings. This allows user-defined formatting to be conveniently coded. The header file *iomanip.h* is also useful for formatting I/O.

C.11.2 Fstream File I/O

In older systems, file I/O was performed using either the C header *stdio.h* or the C++ header *stream.h*. Turbo C++ uses *fstream.h* (see Section 7.5).

File I/O is handled by including *fstream.h*. This contains classes `ofstream` and `ifstream` for output file stream and input file stream creation and manipulation. To properly open and manage an `ifstream` or `ofstream` related to a system file, you first declare them with an appropriate constructor.

```
ifstream();
ifstream(const char*, int = ios::in, int prot = filebuf::openprot);
```

The constructor of no arguments creates a variable that will later on be associated with an input file. The constructor of three arguments takes as its first argument the named file. The second argument specifies the file mode. The third argument is for file protection. These are defined as enumerators in class `ios` as follows:

```
ios::in            //input mode
ios::app           //append mode
ios::out           //output mode
ios::ate           //open and seek to end of file
ios::nocreate      //open but do not create mode
ios::trunc         //discard contents and open
ios::noreplace     //if file exists open fails
```

Thus the default for an `ifstream` is input mode, and for an `ofstream` is output mode. If file opening fails, the value 0 is returned.

It is also possible to create a file that is used for both input and output as follows:

```
fstream in_out("temp", ios::in|ios::out);
```

The file named `temp` is created for both reading and writing.

Some important member functions that are found in *fstream.h* include:

```
//opens ifstream file
void open(const char*, int = ios::in, int prot = filebuf::openprot);

//opens ofstream file
void open(const char*, int = ios::out, int prot = filebuf::openprot);

void close();
```

These functions can be used to open and close appropriate files.

Additional member functions in other I/O classes allow for a full range of file manipulation. For example:

```
//seeks and tells for put
ostream&    seekp(streampos p) ;
ostream&    seekp(streamoff o, seek_dir d) ;
streampos   tellp() ;

//seeks and tells for get
istream&    seekg(streampos p) ;
istream&    seekg(streamoff o, seek_dir d) ;
streampos   tellg() ;
```

The `streampos` value is the current location of either the *get* or *put* position in the file. The `streamoff` value is a relative position in bytes from the current absolute file position. The `seek_dir` value is one of the enumerators:

```
ios::beg    //beginning of the file
ios::cur    //current position
ios::end    //end of the file

//examples
out_f.seekp(5, ios::beg);   //5 bytes from beginning for put
in.seekg(-5, ios::cur);     //5 bytes back for get
```

C.12 Caution and Compatibility

C++ is not completely upward compatible with C. In most cases of ordinary use, it is a superset of C. Also C++ is not a completely stable language design. It is at the beginning of the ANSI standards process and several novel features are being experimented with, most notably exception handling and parameterized types. The following sections mention features of the language that are problematic.

C.12.1 Nested Class Declarations

The original scoping of nested classes was based on C rules. In effect, nesting was cosmetic, with the inner class globally visible. This rule is to be changed with Release 2.1 of the AT&T C++ Language System. The inner class will be local to the outer class enclosing it. Accessing such an inner class could require multiple use of the scope resolution operator.

```
int outer::inner::foo(double w) //foo is nested
    . . .
```

It will also be possible to have classes nested inside functions. To avoid incompatibilities between C++ systems and between C++ and ANSI C, it is best to avoid these forms of nesting.

C.12.2 Type Compatibilities

In general, C++ is more strongly typed than ANSI C. Some differences include:

1. Enumerations are distinct types, with enumerators not being explicitly `int`. This means that enumerations must be cast when making assignments from integer types or other enumerations to each other. They are promotable to integer.

2. Any pointer type can be converted to a generic pointer of type `void*`. However, unlike ANSI C, a generic pointer is not assignment-compatible with an arbitrary pointer type. This means that C++ requires that generic pointers be cast to an explicit type for assignment to a nongeneric pointer variable.

3. In C++, the size of a literal character is the same as `sizeof(char)`. It can store enumeration types in less than `sizeof(int)`. In ANSI C, the size of literal characters and enumeration types is the same as `sizeof(int)`.

C.12.3 Miscellaneous

The old C function syntax where the argument list is left blank is replaced in ANSI C by the explicit argument `void`. The signature `foo()` in C is considered equivalent to the use of ellipsis and in C++ is considered equivalent to the empty argument list.

In early C++ systems, the `this` pointer could be modified. It could be used to allocate memory for class objects. Although this use is obsolete, a compiler can continue to allow it.

C++ allows declarations to be intermixed with executable statements. ANSI C allows declarations to be only at the heads of blocks or in file scope. However in C++, goto, iteration, and selection statements are not allowed to bypass initialization of variables. This rule differs from ANSI C.

In C++, a global data object must have exactly one definition. Other declarations must use the keyword `extern`. ANSI C allows multiple declarations without the keyword `extern`.

C.12.4 Unimplemented Features

The keyword template is reserved to implement parameterized types. Typically, an ADT such as a stack or list is used to store a large number of item values of the same type. Such an ADT is called a container class. Rather than repeatedly recoding for each explicit type, its own class, the template feature allows a general formulation that can be explicitly instantiated for each type.

```
template <class T>       //parameterize T
class stack {
private:
    T*   top;
    int  size;
public:
    stack();
    stack(int s);
    T& pop();
    void push(T);
    ...
};
typedef stack<string> str_stack;
str_stack s(100);    //an explicit variable used as a string stack
```

This is based on a proposal of Bjarne Stroustrup. It may not survive in this form. In many cases it will replace code reuse schemes based on macro expansion or inheritance.

Exception handling using the keywords catch, throw, and try is also proposed.

Appendix D

Turbo C++ Editor Commands

The Turbo C editor commands are grouped into four categories: cursor movement commands, insert and delete commands, block commands, and miscellaneous commands. In the tables that follow, we use ^x to indicate that control-x must be typed, and we use ^xy to indicate that control-xy must be typed. More explicitly, ^xy means that the control key must be held down while typing xy. Some actions can be achieved with more than one editor command. Where appropriate, these alternate commands are listed.

CURSOR MOVEMENT COMMANDS		
Action	Command	Alternate Command
Character left	^s	*Left arrow*
Character right	^d	*Right arrow*
Line up	^e	*Up arrow*
Line down	^x	*Down arrow*
Word left	^a	
Word right	^f	
Beginning of line	^q	*Home*
End of line	^d	*End*
Page up	^r	*Page up*
Page down	^c	*Page down*
Scroll up	^w	
Scroll down	^z	

CURSOR MOVEMENT COMMANDS (cont.)		
Action	**Command**	**Alternate Command**
Top of window	$^\wedge$qe	
Bottom of window	$^\wedge$qx	
Top of file	$^\wedge$qr	
End of file	$^\wedge$qc	
Beginning of block	$^\wedge$qb	
End of block	$^\wedge$qk	
Last cursor position	$^\wedge$qp	

INSERT AND DELETE COMMANDS		
Action	**Command**	**Alternate Command**
Insert mode toggle	$^\wedge$v	*Insert*
Insert line	$^\wedge$n	
Delete character	$^\wedge$g	*Delete*
Delete character to left	$^\wedge$h	*Backspace*
Delete word to right	$^\wedge$t	
Delete line	$^\wedge$y	
Delete to end of line	$^\wedge$qy	

BLOCK COMMANDS	
Action	**Command**
Mark begin block	$^\wedge$kb
Mark end block'	$^\wedge$kk
Mark word	$^\wedge$kt
Copy block	$^\wedge$kc
Delete block	$^\wedge$ky
Move block	$^\wedge$kv
Read block from disk	$^\wedge$kr
Write block to disk	$^\wedge$kw
Hide block toggle	$^\wedge$kh

MISCELLANEOUS COMMANDS		
Action	**Command**	**Alternate Command**
Invoke main menu	*F10*	
Load file	*F3*	
Save file	^ks	*F2*
Quit editor without save	^kd	^kq
Abort operation	^u	
Restore line	^ql	
Find	^qf	
Repeat last find	^i	
Find and replace	^qa	
Autoindent toggle	^oi	
Control character prefix	^p	
Mark place in file	^k *n*	
Find place in file	^q *n*	
Tab	^i	*Tab*
Tab mode toggle	^ot	

Using Edit and Search Menus

The *Edit* menu and the *Search* menu let you easily do many editing functions with the mouse. Many of these commands work with the *Clipboard* window. We describe these facilities as used with a mouse. They are also available from the keyboard.

Text is selected by dragging the mouse cursor over the edit window (working document). The text is highlighted as you drag. A single line can be selected by a double click on any part of that line. Selected text can now be usefully manipulated with the *copy*, *cut*, and *paste* commands. The *copy* command places the selected text into the clipboard window. The *cut* command removes the selected text from the working document and places it in the clipboard. The *paste* command takes the text placed into the clipboard and places it at the cursor position in the working document. The edit window also has a *clear* command that removes selected text without placing it in the clipboard. Therefore, cleared text is not recoverable.

The search menu has *find*, *replace*, *search again*, and *go to line number* commands that are useful when editing. *Find* brings up a dialog box that lets you enter text to be searched for. *Replace* brings up a dialog box that lets you enter text that is to be substituted for. *Search again* allows the previous find or replace command to be repeated. *Go to line number* is self-explanatory.

INDEX

About the Author

Ira Pohl, Ph.D., is a professor of computer and information sciences at the University of California, Santa Cruz. He has two decades of experience as a software methodologist and is an international authority on C and C++ programming. His teaching and research interests include artificial intelligence and programming languages. Professor Pohl has lectured extensively at U.C. Berkeley, the Courant Institute, Edinburgh University, Stanford, and the Vrije University in Amsterdam. He is the author of the best-selling *C++ for C Programmers* and coauthor, with Al Kelley, of a very successful series of C books: *A Book on C: Programming in C, Second Edition; C by Dissection;* and *Turbo C.* When not programming, he enjoys riding bicycles in Aptos, California, with his wife Debra and daughter Laura.